Twentieth-Century Models of the Theatrical Work

KRZYSZTOF
PLEŚNIAROWICZ

Twentieth-Century Models of the Theatrical Work

TRANSLATED BY WILLIAM BRAND

JAGIELLONIAN UNIVERSITY PRESS

REVIEW
Prof. dr hab. Leszek Kolankiewicz

COVER DESIGN
Marta Jaszczuk

On the cover: Angkana (Adobe Stock)

Author's photo by Jan Pleśniarowicz.

This publication was funded by the Faculty of Management and Social Communication at the Jagiellonian University, Institute of Culture

© Copyright by Krzysztof Pleśniarowicz & Jagiellonian University Press
  Translation © William Brand 2018
  The moral right of the translator has been asserted.
  First edition, Kraków 2024
  All rights reserved

This publication is protected by the Polish Act on Copyright and Related Rights. The Publisher—Jagiellonian University Press and other entitled authors, creators, entities are the copyright holders. Copying, distributing and other use of this publication in full or in part without the Publisher's consent is prohibited except for permitted personal and public use or under an open access license granted by the Publisher.

ISBN 978-83-233-5374-4 (print)
ISBN 978-83-233-7557-9 (PDF)
ISBN 978-83-233-7558-6 (epub)
https://doi.org/10.4467/K7557.111/23.24.19238

www.wuj.pl

Jagiellonian University Press
Editorial Offices: Michałowskiego 9/2, 31-126 Kraków, Poland
Phone: +48 12 663 23 80
Distribution: Phone: +48 12 631 01 97
Cell Phone: +48 506 006 674, e-mail: sprzedaz@wuj.pl
Bank: PEKAO SA, IBAN PL 80 1240 4722 1111 0000 4856 3325

CONTENTS

INTRODUCTION: The twentieth-century deconstruction
of the model of theatrical illusion ... 7

THE THEATRICAL BOX OF ILLUSION: A SPACE FOR VISUALIZATION ... 13

Two infinities: The Cartesian *cogito* in the box stage ... 15
The semiotic model: Delsarte's geometry of gestures ... 24
The rhetorical model: Freytag's pyramid ... 33
Mathematical universe ... 40

THE DREAMS OF "INHIBITED PRACTITIONERS" ... 43

The ideal work of the New Theater: Appia's model ... 45
The legacy of symbolism: Artaud's magical model ... 57
The legacy of naturalism: Brecht's ideological model ... 70
Two theaters ... 81

THE PARATHEATRICAL AMBITIONS OF THEORY: FAITH IN THE SPATIALIZATION OF WORDS ... 83

The theater of the structuralists and semioticians:
the temptation of sign processes ... 85
The theater of the phenomenologists—stage and spectacle:
the ceremony of presentation ... 102
The theater of sociologists and anthropologists: the dogma
of convention ... 119
The hope of perfection ... 135

BEYOND UTOPIA AND FAITH: THE SPACE OF ANTI-ILLUSION 137

The deconstruction of representation: Wilson's model 139
The desemanticization of the message: Kantor's model 147
The delimitation of culture: Brook's model 158
Continuity revolutions 167

CONCLUSION: The dimensions of anti-illusion 169

Bibliography 177
Index 187

INTRODUCTION:
The twentieth-century deconstruction of the model of theatrical illusion

"The last 100 years have seen a constant battle against the concept of theatrical illusion: the idea that what we are watching is a plausible reproduction of reality. Everything has conspired against it," wrote Michael Billington in 2012.[1]

The phenomenon of dramatic and theatrical illusion, which was subjected to various forms of deconstruction in the twentieth century, seems to be inextricably bound up with the very European convention of simulating scenes of real life on stage in accordance with the social models and norms accepted at a given moment.

The effectiveness of theatrical illusion in the European theater tradition resulted not so much from the constantly improved, rich repertoire of staging and acting techniques as from, above all, the willingness of spectators to accept the dominant theatrical conventions. At various times, as Pierre Francastel noted, there have been various recipes for creating illusion.[2] The effectiveness of illusion, in painting or the theater, depended after all on the "collectively accepted means of understanding reality."[3] Theatrical illusion depended, as Reginbald A. Foakes wrote,

---

[1] M. Billington, *I Is for illusion*, "The Guardian" (February 8, 2012).
[2] P. Francastel, *La Réalité figurative*, Paris 1965, 224.
[3] Ibid.

on "the activity of mind on the part of the spectator that distinguishes dramatic illusion from scenic illusion."[4]

In his French *Dictionnaire du Théâtre* [Dictionary of Theatrical Terms], Patrice Pavis put forward just such a definition:

> "We are dealing with theatrical illusion when the beholder treats as the real world that which is only fiction, and therefore the result of the artistic creation of the presented world. Illusion is connected with the effect of reality produced through the stage and with the process of the recognition by the beholder of the observed world as his own, where things occur in conformity to his experience and convictions."[5]

The fullest manifestation of the theater of total illusion was the naturalistic convention of the "fourth stage wall" at the end of the nineteenth century, permanently dividing two worlds—the theatrical work and the audience, who for the first time sat in the dark. Total illusion was assumed by the theater of August Strindberg, among others. As J. L. Styan encapsulates this postulate: "His audience was to be completely convinced of the reality of the world of the stage and transported wholly into its sphere of influence."[6]

Reginald A. Foakes insightfully noted that the main drawback of theatrical naturalism was the assumption of the full engagement of the beholder in a "magic world of illusion" as a result of being turned into a "voyeur"—without there being any "necessary connection between that scenic or outward illusion, and the freeing of the imagination that encourages what Coleridge called 'inner illusion.'"[7] An important theoretical reformer of the theater at the turn of the nineteenth and twentieth centuries, Edward Gordon Craig, discerned this shortcoming. As early as 1909, he referred to naturalism in the theater—from Irving through Antoine to Stanislavski—as a "new artificiality."[8]

---

[4] R. A. Foakes, *Making and Breaking Dramatic Illusion*, in: *Aesthetic Illusion Theoretical and Historical Approaches*, ed. F. Burwick, W. Pape, Berlin and New York 1990, 217.

[5] P. Pavis, *Dictionnaire du Théâtre*, Paris 1980, 209.

[6] J. L. Styan, *Modern Drama in Theory and Practice*, Vol. 1: *Realism and Naturalism*, Cambridge 1986, 43.

[7] R. A. Foakes, *Making and Breaking...*, 225.

[8] Ibid.

From that time on there were increasing calls for the theater—and the audience—to be liberated from that artificiality of illusion, which had been a part of European art for centuries in "the Great Tradition of Illusionism."[9] The change would have to involve an altered definition of the theatrical work, subordinated to new anti-illusionistic rules and examples. There would have to be a renunciation of the simple equation of the stage and the real world, in favor of many equally entitled, evenly matched worlds evoked in an unending cycle.

As Austin E. Quigley, who studied *Other Worlds* in the twentieth-century theater put it: "In the modern period, a second world is important not just for the relationship it contracts with a first world, but because its very existence as a second world suggests the possibility of others."[10]

It is no accident that theoretical divagations on the effervescent and thorny subject of the theatrical play have often taken the form of models, be they graphic, mathematical or symbolic. Attempts have been made in this way to support definitions or hierarchical arrangements of theatrical phenomena according to various assumptions. Such attempts create neither a realistic image of the theater nor fictions useful in analysis—as described by Ian G. Barbour in reference to the humanities—but rather partial and provisional ways of imagining an unobservable reality.[11]

The fact that metatheatrical reflections in the twentieth century tend to be models results from the necessity to make some order of experience (the performance and reception of the theatrical work), and not from the nature of the phenomenon (the autonomous theatrical work) being described. It seems that the questions formulated by Roland Barthes at the beginning of the 1960s are still pertinent today. And that they demand answers—or rather models.

"What is theater?" Barthes asked himself, and replied:

> "A kind of cybernetic machine. When it is not working, this machine is hidden behind a curtain. But as soon as it is revealed, it begins emitting a certain number of messages. These messages have this peculiarity, that they are simultaneous and

---

[9] W. Wolf, *Illusion and Breaking Illusion in Twentieth-Century Fiction*, in: *Aesthetic Illusion Theoretical and Historical Approaches*, ed. F. Burwick, W. Pape, Berlin and New York 1990, 284.

[10] A. E. Quigley, *The Modern Stage and Other Worlds*, New York and London 1985, 260.

[11] I. G. Barbour, *Myths, Models and Paradigms: A Comparative Study in Science and Religion*, New York 1974.

yet of different rhythm . . . what we have, then, is a real informational polyphony, which is what theatricality is: *a density of signs*...What relations do these counterpointed signs . . . have among themselves? They do not have the same signifiers [*signifiants*] (by definition); but do they always signify the same thing [*signifié*]? Do they combine in a single meaning? . . . Further, how is the theatrical signifier formed? What are its models?"[12]

The present work makes a critical comparison of, on the one hand, my selected reconstructions of "signifying" (or "presenting") models in the contemporary theory of the theater. Models created (or dreamed of) by theatrical practitioners, beginning at the turn of the nineteenth and twentieth centuries, as well as schemes elaborated by theoreticians—semiologists, phenomenologists, and anthropologists—less closely connected with actual practice.

As models, the theses of the New Theater propounded since the end of the nineteenth century (the outstanding writing about the theater by Appia, Artaud, and Brecht) determined the practice of twentieth-century stagecraft. To this day, these models are the basis for much of the theoretical reflection on the theater. They also figure in the academic discussions around the theater, inspired by theoreticians of the semiotics of culture, the phenomena of interpersonal presence, and social and artistic conventions.

It is possible in each case to speak of the spatial understanding of the theatrical work. In the opinion of Regis Durand, it is precisely the spatial quality of theater art that is the indicator of theatricality: "It balances out the influence of linearity (and temporality) introduced by literature."[13]

The geometrical conventions of the indestructible box stage, discovered during the Renaissance and Baroque periods and subjected to the cycles of the permanent aesthetic revolution in the twentieth century, are a constant reference point for the analyses in this book. So are the "geometrization" of the canons of acting and the rules of dramatic action. The "anti-illusionist spaces" of the greatest artists of the stage at the end of the twentieth century, Robert Wilson, Tadeusz Kantor, and

---

[12] R. Barthes, *Critical Essays*, trans. R. Howard, Evanston 1972, 261–262.

[13] R. Durand, *Problemes de l'analyse structurale et sémiotique de la forme théâtrale*, in: A. Helbo and others, *Sémiologie de la représentation. Théâtre, télévision, bande dessinée*, Bruxelles 1975, 113.

Peter Brook, are points of departure. The plays are models of the "new theatricality," no longer inhering in manifestos or dissertations but in the living material of performance (placed in the context of the latest aesthetic transformations of art, and not only the art of the theater).

Models of the theatrical work invented or created in the last century, still relevant, attempt to resolve the contradictions that naturally arise from the characteristics of the box stage: "a box for viewing." From today's perspective, the competing and changing visions of the art of theater turn out to have more in common than differences.

THE THEATRICAL BOX OF ILLUSION:
A SPACE FOR VISUALIZATION

TWO INFINITIES:
THE CARTESIAN *COGITO* IN THE BOX STAGE

The invention during the Renaissance of the modern box (from the German *Guckkasten*, literally a "looking box") or Italian (*à l'italienne*) stage and its development in the Baroque period were closely connected with the dominance at the time of a view of the world based on painting. The vital optical connection between the spectator's eye and the three-dimensional stage image appeared from the start to be an attractive solution to the basically mathematical problem posed for painting by the greatest artists of the time: how to integrate the space of the image on the basis of the principle of the objective reproduction of perceived, physical reality.

To this day, that stage, *boîte à miracles*, which transforms the theater into an ever more effective optical box, inscribes the Euclidean visual pyramid (following Alberti's treatise on painting) in theatrical space, remains the most perfect manifestation of the Renaissance belief that the world is geometrical in form, and that nature itself is unchanging, subject to mathematical rules and accessible to man in the form of a spectacle at once true and fleeting, like the image conjured up in a *camera obscura*.

Alberti wrote in 1435:

> "... it is said that vision makes a triangle. The base of [this triangle] is the quantity seen and the sides are those rays which are extended from the quantity to the eye. It is, therefore, very certain that no quantity can be seen without the triangle. The angles in this visual triangle are first, the two points of the quantity, the third, that which is opposite the base and located within the eye."[14]

---

[14] L. B. Alberti, *On Painting*, New Haven 1970, 46.

This was not, of course, the sole model of the theater in the sixteenth and seventeenth centuries: it persisted and developed in opposition to the still vital medieval, Shakesperean, and popular tradition (*commedia dell'arte*). Without repeating all that has been written copiously and in detail on this subject, it is perhaps worth reminding ourselves about the direction in which the new invention developed, between the architectonic-symbolic Vitruvian and the painterly-illusionist anti-Vitruvian concepts. Between the actor-centered theater that highlights the word, without decoration and machinery, and the decorative theater that aims for the Renaissance form of the total spectacle. Between the theater of the opened space and the theater enclosed in the box of a chamber.[15]

The discoverers of the box launched a true festival of spectacular illusion, based on the ever more perfect technology of *repraesentatio*. Rudolf Arnheim has emphasized that there was "a scientifically oriented preference for mechanical reproduction and geometrical constructs in place of creative imagery."[16] This is surely why the great painters rejected the theater just as quickly as they had conquered it, abandoning it to theatrical artisans who bedazzled audiences not so much with their artistic conception as with their technical ingenuity.[17]

Quickly abandoned by the great painters, the stage remained for the next three centuries in thrall to the rigors of pure science, algebra, geometry, and perspective that they had introduced.

No longer was the world only copied allegorically (as on the simultaneous medieval stage) or on the static-illusionist stage (as in the *picturae scenae*, also patterned on painting). The chance to freely shape the space confined within the frame of the stage—in a deliberate allusion to rediscovered ancient techniques (the *telari* system) and in the development of ever more ingenious machinery (based on a new backstage system), increasingly meticulously prepared decorations, and finally variable

---

[15] See D. Ratajczak, *Przestrzeń w dramacie i dramat w przestrzeni teatru*, Poznań 1985, 40–41.
[16] R. Arnheim, *Art and Visual Perception: A Psychology of the Creative Eye*, Berkeley and Los Angeles 1974, 284.
[17] Z. Raszewski, *Przedmowa*, in: J. Furttenbach, *O budowie teatrów*, trans. Z. Raszewski, Wrocław 1958, 10.

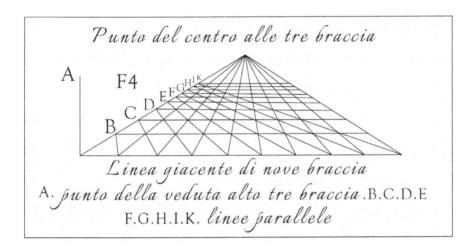

Figure 1. Alberti: The Visual Pyramid (*Della Pittura*, 1435)

and ever-more effective artificial illumination—was increasingly, and successfully exploited.[18]

The turn of the nineteenth and twentieth centuries brought theatrical illusionism to a close: "The painted backdrop was replaced by neutral canvas, highlighted with electric lamps in a way that convincingly imitated the color effects of our atmosphere. Three-dimensional décor was hung against this background, lighted in an extraordinarily clever way … going any further was not possible."[19] Yet at the beginning of the twentieth century, the centuries-long process of making the theater resemble a painting was brought to a close, and what is more it turned out to be the principal argument for implementing the reform of the theater after 1880: "The stage opening through which one can look after the raising of the curtain, formed according to the painterly principles of illusionistic decoration, was the object of the fiercest attacks in the polemics of the reformers."[20]

New aesthetic criteria determined the temperature of those polemics, but the fundamental meaning of the New Theater depended above all on the increasing acceptance of a way of depicting the world different from the mathematical-geometrical one.

> "Central perspective produces a mathematically accurate but psycho-physiologically impossible representation of space," wrote Arnold Hauser. "This completely rationalized conception could appear to be the adequate reproduction of the actual optical impression only to such a thoroughly scientific period as the centuries between the Renaissance and the end of the nineteenth century. Uniformity and consistency were in fact the highest criteria of truth during the whole of this period."[21]

The domination of sensory illusion over the drama of the interpersonal; the homogeneity of the mathematical model over the lack of continuity of real perception; mechanical reproduction creative imagination—these are not the only paradoxes of the wondrous invention that prevailed in European theater from the seventeenth to the twentieth centuries.

---

[18] See D. Ratajczak, *Przestrzeń w dramacie...*, 22; M. Berthold, *A History of World Theater*, New York 1972, 420–425.

[19] Z. Raszewski, *Przedmowa*, 9.

[20] Ibid., 7.

[21] A. Hauser, *The Social History of Art*, Vol. 2: *Renaissance, Mannerism, Baroque*, London and New York 1999, 69.

Two infinities: The Cartesian *cogito* in the box stage

Dobrochna Ratajczak[22] catalogues them differently. The power of illusionistic, painterly decoration and the tempting magic of perspective bore fruit in the paradox of the open within the enclosed, that is the revealing of the open landscape in what is after all the delimited box of the stage. Thanks to the constant improvement of technical solutions, the possibility of forming a profusion of the places where things occurred was created, which meant not only breaking with the principal of the unity of place, but also the creation up of another paradox—unity in multiplicity (or the unity of the box stage and the plurality of places conjured up in a painterly way).

Ratajczak attributed this new concept of the *theatrum mundi* to both the broad-scale use of parts to suggest a whole (within the limited box model of the world) and the whole suggesting a part (the assumption of a human dimension to the world, according to the laws of vision). And also the antinomies of secularity (designating a safe distance for the passive spectator-observer) and sanctity (or the maintenance of the sacral in terms of pedigree and the division into stage and audience). It is worth adding to this list the collision between centrality and infinity—concepts that have been contraries since antiquity.

As Rudolf Arnheim wrote:

> "The notion that not only God is infinite, as the philosophers of the Middle Ages had maintained, but that the world is infinite as well is a conception of the Renaissance age . . . central perspective portraits space as a flow oriented toward a specified end. It thereby transforms the timeless simultaneity of traditional, undeformed space into a happening in time—that is, a directed sequence of events The world of being is redefined as a process of happening."[23]

Concealed behind these spatial paradoxes of the stage *á l'italienne*, which determined its attractiveness for the majority of post-Renaissance theatrical conventions, was a fundamental conflict that could not be solved as long as perspective was calling the shots: Where, with space and time settled, did the actor, along with the character he created, fit into the overall structure of mathematical truth. In Dobrochna Ratajczak's words, "the Italian stage was subjected to the painterly rules for the construction of an

---

[22] See D. Ratajczak, *Przestrzeń w dramacie...*, 29.
[23] R. Arnheim, *Art and Visual Perception...*, 298.

image that possessed as its foundation a 'mathematical code,' a keystone of the objective perfection of the world and the objective perfection of its image."[24] On the new box stage, progressively and dynamically subjugated to the scientific rules of the painting of the day the theatrical space "as the element of appearance and the substratum of sense experience" becomes unquestionably dominant "over the substantiality of man and allows the human figure to be absorbed by space."[25]

As Zbigniew Raszewski wrote,

> "the dictatorship of theatrical perspective became so ruthless that in the end nothing was left for the actor but a narrow strip on the very edge of the platform, because if he dared to wander into the upstage depths then the house painted in perspective would only come up to his waist. That house painted in perspective seemed to everyone, however, to be something so precious and indispensable that instead of simply throwing it out of the theater, an effort was made to show children in the depths of the stage who were costumed and made up exactly the same as the actors proper were costumed. And thus the child in the depths was shown at one point, and then its adult doppelganger at the front of the stage."[26]

The "painting in motion" favored spatial illusion over the human image and the spectator over the actor, while replacing the development of verbal action which shifts of place. "Theater eclipsed drama."[27] Thus was revealed a conflict between the rhythmic order of the anthropocentric perspective on the one hand and the arrhythmia of the actions and feelings of dramatic protagonists enmeshed in the unpredictability of the "interpersonal" on the other.

Yet as early as the seventeenth century this conflict found sanction in Cartesian dualism. The geometrical box stage, it turned out, could be excellent proof of the self-fulfilling "argument from illusion." According to J. L. Austin: "In fact, of course, our senses are dumb—though Descartes and others speak of 'the testimony of the senses', our senses do not *tell* us anything, true or false."[28] The actor, in turn, by carrying the circle of his own consciousness into the illusional space, supplies metaphysical

---

[24] D. Ratajczak, *Przestrzeń w dramacie...*, 37.
[25] A. Hauser, *The Social History...*, 124.
[26] Z. Raszewski, *Przedmowa*, 11.
[27] D. Ratajczak, *Przestrzeń w dramacie...*, 30.
[28] J. L. Austin, *Sense and Sensibilia*, reconstructed from manuscript notes by G. J. Warnock, Oxford 1962, 11.

proof, a sign of that substantial soul with the sole attribute of thinking, and which is identical with thinking (as is known, thinking is the only thing that the Cartesian subject can be sure of, and not be wrong about).

Daniel Dennett described Cartesian theater thus:

> "We seem to imagine that there is some place inside 'my' mind or brain where 'I' am. This place has something like a mental screen or stage on which images are presented for viewing by my mind's eye. In this special place everything that we are conscious of at a given moment comes together and consciousness happens. The ideas and feelings that are in this place are *in consciousness*, and all the rest are unconscious. The show in the Cartesian theater is the stream of consciousness, and the audience is me."[29]

When he was led out onto the proscenium (endangering the perspective principle of the theatrical picture), the lone actor acquired an exceptional opportunity: isolated from the making present of the outer world feigned through the senses and appearances of things, he could enunciate the truth of the second theater all the more fully. This was the inner theater, existing in the conscious acts of the Cartesian *cogito* and resistant to the illusionistic making present of the external theater. (Corneille thought that the entire action of his tragedies took place in the soul of the heroes).

The actor—authorized to represent, in words, acts of the experience of self-awareness, and thus of the second type of perception accessible to people—was, in accordance with the principle of Cartesian dualism, an expression of objection to the traditional spiritual-physical unity, an expression of the freeing of the consciousness—identified with the soul—from the mortal body. It was thus an expression of the idea of the infinity and limitless of human thought that was inscribed in the concept of *cogito*.

Both infinities, the one resulting from the geometry of central perspective and the one contained in the idea of the infallibility of the "internal point of view" of the central self, share an identical subordination to mathematical ideas. Descartes analyzed that inner theater (in conformity with the tenets of his philosophy) according to the perfect pattern he discerned in the geometrical system, the same one that suggested the modern concept of the stage image.

---

[29] D. Dennett, *Consciousness Explained*, Boston 1991, 65.

This is how the Cartesian *cogito* made it possible to reconcile the initial antinomy between the geometrical illusion box and the feeling, thinking human actor who threatened its rules—who from that moment on could be regarded as an equal ingredient in a world under the sway of mathematics. Thanks to the concept of the autonomous *cogito*, the theatrical space of pictures in motion could thus become subjective. It was at this time that action in the sphere of the illusory world took on the characteristics of real theatricality, because it made it possible to perceive not the world itself, but the mental state and actions of the intellectually active protagonist.

Propagated together with Cartesian doctrine, the conception of two theaters, mutually complementary, internal, and external, along with that philosopher's proposed method of transcending the *cogito*, determined not only the relations between staging and action, between theatrical event and audience in Western theater,[30] but also the development of Western forms on the box stage.

After all, modern drama is built on this tension between the external world as a source of conflicts and complications, and the internal world that is made present in acts of self-awareness (hence the popularity, which grew until the time of naturalism, of the monologue as an expression of the protagonist's solitude)—in other words, on the tension between what is commonly known as the interior life of the protagonist and his existence among other characters, between the theater of characters and the theater of action.

Various detailed outcomes were possible here. "And so, for example," Dobrochna Ratajczak has written,

> "Racine's tragedy treats space as a 'blind nexus' in relation to the text, based on an intimate spatial horizon brought onto the stage by particular characters. The genres of opera and melodrama, in turn, treat space as a surrounding for the characters, serving as a background to them and appearing in the role of an important partner for the events presented. Bourgeois drama takes yet another approach to space, initiating the process (completed at the end of the nineteenth century) of the increasingly tight roping together of character and space: the character might endow space with particular, unique traits, but space can also practically call into

---

[30] See S. J. Tharu, *The Sense of Performance: Studies in Post-Artaud Theatre*, New Delhi 1984, 16–19.

being characters inscribed in some way in space, dependent upon space—as can be observes … in naturalistic drama."[31]

The evolving changes in the relation between the theatrical space and the characters acting there significantly enhanced the significance of the playwright—not only as the constructor of dramatic form but also as the external arbiter who was more important than the decorator or the stage technician. Opting for the literary nature of the theater made possible not only the further development of theatrical genres, but also a departure from the principle of changing the text being produced for the sake of various historical stage conventions. Therefore, after a short period in which the perspective stage was turned over to painters exploring the idea of spatial infinity, the new discovered magical box quickly became nothing more than a convenient machine for spatializing literature and seeking the infinite in man.

The theater of pictures in motion returned to being dramatic art.

---

[31] D. Ratajczak, *Przestrzeń w dramacie…*, 63.

THE SEMIOTIC MODEL: DELSARTE'S GEOMETRY OF GESTURES

The antinomy between symmetry and asymmetry and the antinomy between eternal order and mundane movement seem to be the principal semantic markers of the development of the Italian stage.[32] To the degree that a clear arrangement with a single axis and a tendency toward the center was obligatory in the renaissance box, the baroque box was based on two optical axes (in accordance with the evolution of the painterly theory of perceiving the world) and introduced episodic multiple-image composition. Thus it stripped space of its Renaissance homogeneity. Achieving the technical perfection of theatrical optics and the technique of open change, Romanticism in turn opted for multiple-stage three dimensionality, which also included the doubling of the scenic frame (on the principle of the window-within-a-window).

Over time, the asymmetric symbolism of spatial relations became common. This consisted of linking characters to a designated place and direction of action. As Dobrochna Ratajczak has written:

> "A network of asymmetrical symbolic meanings, referring to the dualistic organization of space [and] the reflex of archaic myth and drama, was laid over the purely painterly technical error of the symmetry of the image. The basic sense was designated here by a network of spatial oppositions: top/bottom, left/right, near/far, [and] central/peripheral, referring to elementary human experience."[33]

A special, asymmetric aspect was brought in by the well-known division between stage right (*côté cour*, the court side, designating the good or the "expressive or active side"), and stage left (*côté jardin*, the garden side,

---

[32] See J. Duvignaud, A. Veinstein, *Le théâtre*, Paris 1976, 81–85.
[33] See D. Ratajczak, *Przestrzeń w dramacie...*, 33, 57.

The semiotic model: Delsarte's geometry of gestures

the "side of identification" of the spectator with the protagonist—also designating evil; toward the end of the eighteenth century a revolutionary reversal of these values occurred).[34]

The antinomies mentioned so far, which after all have never been fully dispelled, strictly connected the principle of perspective—or a certain "immobile" order of the construction of spatial significances (within the scope of the symmetrical backstage perspective)—and the inevitable undermining of the symmetrical equilibrium by the living, moving actor. More precisely, by the network of symbolic meanings (for example the semiotic space of gesture) asymmetrically shaped by the actor.

The aspiration toward homogenizing man and space, reconciling the fundamental contradiction inscribed in the nature of the box stage—the eternal competition played out between asymmetry and symmetry in "pictures in motion"—remained even when the stage was left empty or "poor." Stripped indeed of painterly decoration but retaining the symmetry of a rectangular box shape, it was threatened by the intrusion of actors asymmetrical in their corporeality and their movements.

The drive to subordinate the actor to the rules of the geometrical box model ripened over a long period into the systematic study of acting technique and playing conventions. Despite the codification by Jean Noverre in the eighteenth century of the ballet dancer's gestures, despite the fixing in tradition of the varied gestures for tragic and comic roles, the contradictions were not eliminated. Even Lessing, fantasizing over a handbook for actors, wrote that "the mechanical adoption of the position of the body, its movements and the auditory conditions of speech, an adoption nevertheless based on irrefutable rules, is the only method of teaching the art of acting."[35]

Those rules were furnished by the French dancing master and theoretician of acting, François Delsarte, who took up the challenge of capturing all the actor's possible behaviors—vocalization, gestures, and motions—within a network of precision codes. Delsarte himself referred to the system that he developed between 1839 and 1859 (published

---

[34] See E. H. Gombrich, *Art and Illusion: A Study in the Psychology of Pictorial Représentation*, London 1960.

[35] G. E. Lessing, *Theatralische Bibliothek* (1754), quoted in: S. Wołkoński, *Człowiek wyrazisty. Sceniczne wychowanie gestu (według Delsarte'a)*, Warszawa 1920, 29.

after the master's death in 1871 on the basis of his pupils' reports) as "semiotics" or "the study of gesture from the point of view of expression—as an external sign corresponding to one or another state of the soul." He was concerned with creating a universal system of knowledge on the subject of "the direct human language": not a system of made-up gestures (as in pantomime), but rather those thanks to which "nature expresses externally ... human impressions, thoughts, and impulses."[36] Delsarte attempted to apply the Ciceronian *significatio* (as opposed to *demonstratio*) to acting.

One of the important exponents of what came to be called Delsartism was Prince Sergey Volkonsky (active in the Russian theater and, from 1921, as an *émigré*), the author of works including the 1913 *Vyrazitel'nyi Chelovek* [The Expressive Person: A Stage Training in Gesture According to Delsarte], which influenced the theory and practice of such figures as Konstantin Stanislavski, Yevgeny Vakhtangov, Mikhail Chekhov, and Vsevolod Meyerhold. Following Delsarte, Volkonsky wrote that:

1. Gesture can be studied from the point of view of expression as an external sign corresponding to a spiritual state; this is Semiotics.
2. It can be studied from the point of view of those laws governing the balance of the human body: this is Statics.
3. It can be studied from the point of view of those laws governing the sequence and alternation of movement: this is Dynamics.[37]

Delsarte's system, taken to be a synonym for mechanical, arbitrary expression through gesture, was in fact—in reaction against the formal training of actors at the time[38]—a deliberate "return to nature" and a call to observe and codify spontaneous human actions and gestures in various situations, because those gestures were "produced" not by aesthetic conventions, but rather by instincts and emotions.

Delsarte and his pupils drew their arguments not only from observing real life, but also from the examples provided by great sculpture and painting—which suggested, for example, the asymmetrical (!) formula

---

[36] Ibid., 44–45.

[37] S. Volkonsky, 61–62, quoted in: R. Whyman, *The Stanislavsky System of Acting: Legacy and Influence in Modern Performance*, Cambridge 2011, 125.

[38] M. Carlson, *Theories of the Theatre*, Ithaka and London 1989, 218.

The semiotic model: Delsarte's geometry of gestures

of the law of counterbalance ("the essence of all rest") as the basic law of human statics:

> "The equilibrium of the body in motion is built on counterbalance, if not always on counterweight, then always on visual counterbalance.... The law of counterbalance depends on the fact that the parts of the human body are arranged in such a way that their directions are constantly opposite: head up—hands down; hand to the right—head to the left; right leg forward—right hand back; left hip raised—left shoulder lowered."[39]

The striking thing about these formulations is their kinship with *The Treatise on Painting* by Leonardo da Vinci who, as we know, invented the rotating stage at the court of Milan in 1496. For example,

> "If the figure rests upon one foot, the shoulder on that side will always be lower than the other; and the pit of the neck will fall perpendicularly over the middle of that leg which supports the body. The same will happen in whatever other view we see that figure, when it has not the arm much extended, nor any weight on its back, in its hand, or on its shoulder, and when it does not, either behind or before, throw out that leg which does not support the body."[40]

Volkonsky wrote about the concurrence between Leonardo's theses and Delsarte's explanations: "[At] times one experiences an unpleasant sensation. There cannot [however] be talk of any sort of borrowing."[41]

Delsarte's "laws of dynamics," or laws of motion, had similar pedigrees in painting and sculpture. First came the principle of succession—"the facial expression precedes the gesture, and the gesture precedes the word." Second was the principle of direction—"the gesture obtains its significance in dependence on the starting point." Third was the principle of the priority of the organs of motion, justifying the rejection of the simultaneity of movements and the "play of the face." The fourth principle, finally, was the harmony of motion—"dynamic richness is the result of the number of joints put in motion; the fewer joints in motion, the more the person comes to resemble a dummy."[42]

Delsarte's system of semiotics turned out in practice to be an analysis of the significatory sensitivity of "all parts of the body" (which means, in

---

[39] S. Wołkoński, *Człowiek wyrazisty...*, 88.
[40] Leonardo da Vinci, *The Treatise on Painting*, London 1877, 32.
[41] S. Wołkoński, *Człowiek wyrazisty...*, 49.
[42] Ibid., 111.

turn, the eye, mouth, nose, head, neck, back, trunk, arm, wrist [hand], and leg) in arrangements of "triplicate triplets" or "nonatones" (nine varieties of movement: a. eccentric-eccentric, concentric-eccentric, normal-eccentric; b. concentric-concentric, eccentric-concentric, normal-concentric; and c. concentric-normal, eccentric-normal, and normal-normal.

Considering the body as an instrument of expression, Delsarte distinguished three zones:

> "The head and neck being the mental zone; the torso, the spiritual-emotional zone; the abdomen and hips, the physical zone. The arms and legs are our contact with the outer world-but the arms, being attached to the torso, take on a predominantly spiritual-emotional quality; the legs, being attached to the heavy lower trunk, take on a predominantly physical quality. Each part of the body subdivides again into the same three zones; in the arm, for instance, the heavy upper arm, physical; the forearm, spiritual-emotional; the hand, mental. In the leg: thigh, physical; foreleg, spiritual-emotional; foot, mental."[43]

These assumptions gave rise to an exceptionally refined analyses of the significance of a variety of gestural variants (detailed and complex) and, as an accompaniment to these analyses, multistory "tables of meaning." What was born of these opinions about the mechanical and arbitrary nature of the system seems to this day to be an incomparable model for the contemporary, semiotic systematization of gestures in the theater and in everyday life.

The analysis of works of art by pupils of Delsarte with the use of these tables revealed the following practical guidelines for actors: In Michaelangelo's frescoes in the Sistine Chapel, the "eccentric-normal" God the Father, representing "expansiveness" or "the giving of life," contrasts with the "normal-normal" hand of Adam ("liberty" or "submission"). The "normal-eccentric" pose of the Belvedere Apollo at the Vatican (with the arrangement of the feet signifying "exaltation," "expansiveness") collides with the "eccentric-normal" version of the Apollo from the Louvre ("indecisively" in mid-step).[44]

Yet Delsarte's semiotic system was not limited to the universalization of the rules for the actor's behavior in space, in an analogy to the examples of painting or sculpture. It was born out of romantic ambition of

---

[43] Delsarte quoted in: R. Arnheim, *Art and Visual Perception...*, 405.
[44] S. Wołkoński, *Człowiek wyrazisty...*, 78, 82, 86–87.

encompassing and summing up the entire cognitive process. The system was intended to be built on the triadic principle, "which can be applied to everything that exists in the world." The concept of the "trinity" was not, however, a direct borrowing from Christian dogma. Delsarte is said to have told Victor Cousin that "It is not Religion that led me to Art, but rather Art that led me to Religion."[45]

And so the "formulas of the human trinity" according to Delsarte were: Mind, Soul, and Life, creating the "triple triad" known as the "nonatone" (life combines within itself mind and soul; the soul—mind and life; and life—the mind and the soul).[46] The language of Life was to be the voice, the language of the Mind—the word; the language of Feelings—the movements of the body.

This somewhat vague metaphysics nevertheless has a clear geometrical core.

> "Everything in the world, whether physical or moral, or in the phenomena of their action—everything is subject to a division into the Normal, Eccentric, and Concentric. . . . Man is at the crossroads, and all movements are carried out either within the horizontal boundaries of the hemispheres—Right and Left, or within the vertical boundaries of the hemispheres—Upper and Lower, and they cannot be other than either from within or from without."[47]

Delsarte assumed that each person is a sort of center of a non-existing circle or sphere, and acts centrifugally (outward from the center), centripetally (inward towards the center) or in a state of equilibrium (centered in himself). Therefore life (and also the voice) is centrifugal; spirit (and thus the movements of the body as well) is normal. Thought (and thus speech as well) is centripetal. "The entire universe of geometry, in which the actions of the three fundamental elements—Life, Thought, and Feelings—are laid out, is arrayed in an arrangement of divisions—Concentric, Eccentric, and Normal"[48] (in a nonatone configuration, of course!).

Delsarte encompassed his analysis of the form of movement in a geometrical figure composed of a circle, four diameters, and four semicircular

---

[45] Delsarte quoted in: O. Aslan, *l'Acteur au XXe siècle*, Paris 1974, 46.
[46] S. Wołkoński, *Człowiek wyrazisty...*, 36–38.
[47] Ibid., 42.
[48] Ibid.

segments. In his opinion, it was exactly this graphic model that could unite "all the variations of the expressive gesture." It was therefore called the "key to all gestures."[49]

This "key" touches in an obvious way on the sources of modern theater, born out of the mathematical rules of perspective. In the history of theater it is yet another—and the most systematic!—expression of the faith that it is possible to capture the semantic order of the "language of the body" in space, that it is possible to eliminate the element of chance in the actor's presence on stage and replace it with clarity of expression, and finally that it is possible to integrate the human ingredient of the performance into the order of the entire world as established within the rules of a spatial, moving image endowed with a universal system of significances.

This is where Delsarte meets the prophet of the stage *à l'italienne*, Vitruvius himself, whose image of man in a square or in a circle became a popular way of expressing the relation of the microcosm to the macrocosm in the Italian Renaissance.[50]

Delsarte's "circle of gestures" was accompanied by the following explication:

> "The vertical line 1 (from top to bottom) expresses affirmation, confirmation; 2, the horizontal line, expresses negation. The oblique lines, 3 and 4, from within outward and from without inward, express rejection. 4, an oblique line from within outward rejects things which we despise. 3, a line from within outward, rejects things which oppress us and of which we wish to get rid. 5, the quadrant of a circle, whose form recalls that of a hammock, expresses well-being, contentment, confidence and happiness. 6, a similar quadrant of a circle, an eccentric curvilinear, ex-presses secrecy, silence, domination, persuasion, stability, imposition, inclosure. The reentering external curvilinear quadrant of a circle, 7, expresses graceful, delicate things. Produced in two ways, from above downward, it expresses physical delicacy; from below upward, moral and intellectual delicacy. The external quadrant of a circle, 8, expresses exuberance and plenitude, amplitude and generosity. The circular line surrounding and embracing is characteristic of glorification and exaltation."[51]

---

[49] Ibid., 100–101. See A. Giraudet, *Mimique, physionomie et geste*, Paris 1895.
[50] See F. A. Yates, *The Art of Memory*, London 1992, 297–298.
[51] F. Delsarte, *Literary Remains of F. Delsarte*, in: *Delsarte System of Oratory*, New York 1893, 498–499.

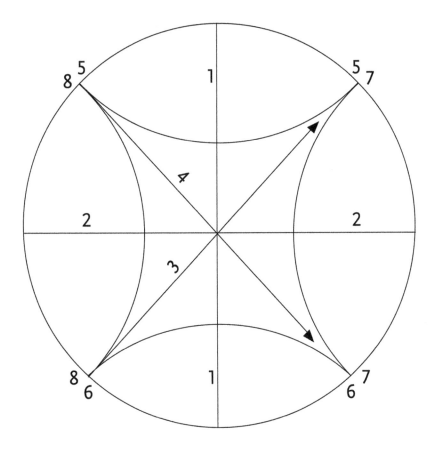

Figure 2. Delsarte: The Key to All Gestures*

---

* A. Giraudet, *Mimique, physionomie…*

But the clear semiotic asymmetry concealed in that model which aspires to symmetry seems to be more interesting than the semiotic version of "all gestures" presented here. It consists of a tendency toward the left side—as shown by both directions of rejection (3 and 4) as well as the semantic predominance of line 7, with its double significance (moral and physical, depending on the direction), and on line 8, which has no corresponding differentiation.

The circle—or sphere—of gestures inscribed in the cube of the illusionary stage, reconciling the inevitable asymmetry of the actor's behavior with his symmetrical image (nevertheless underlain with asymmetry) was intended to guarantee the integrity of the re-presented image of the "real" world. And so too the subjection of acting to the scientific precision of cognition and that "mechanical skill" postulated by Lessing. "Faithfulness to nature—that is what lies of the basis of that 'skill' taught by Delsarte," writes Volkonsky, "Faithfulness to nature, and now faithfulness with the established 'customs and manners of the stage.'"[52]

It would seem that the System described here, to which all twentieth-century acting methods more or less consciously referred (Grotowski spoke directly about "Delsarte's study of the concentric and eccentric reactions in Human behavior"[53]), was the last meeting place of the two great utopias of the modern theater, expressed in the slogans of naturalism and symbolism, aiming at making present the "truth" about the world (in accordance with the principles of that world). And thus both the utopia of the directness of the illusionistic experience of the mirror of reality, and the utopia of the indirect conveyance of that which is close to the essence of things, while nevertheless being simply inaccessible to the senses.

From the turn of the 19th and 20th centuries these have been mutually exclusive slogans that divide the development of the contemporary theater into two parallel currents that would never again be able to converge.

---

[52] S. Wołkoński, *Człowiek wyrazisty...*, 117.
[53] See O. Aslan, *l'Acteur au XXe siècle*; J. Grotowski, *Teksty z lat 1965–1969*, Wrocław 1989, 8.

THE RHETORICAL MODEL: FREYTAG'S PYRAMID

An important difference between regular and irregular genres emerged from the beginning within the space of the box stage. The former (comedy, tragedy) maintained the dominance of the word in the conventional acting space (as in Serlia's concept from 1545: a square with streets in perspective for comedy or a temple-palace complex for tragedy). The place for the staging of regular genres on the *l'italienne* stage was "transparent": the play was presented separately and the decoration existed separately. In turn, the irregular genres (referred to as "intermediate," which over time became increasingly significant—such as opera, drama, tragicomedy, or melodrama) treated visual perception as being on an equal footing, or even as having the highest priority.

For those irregular genres, the box stage was an ideal machine for conjuring up an illusory, visual world. The image, the visual presentation, the *repraesentatio*, turned out to be more important than the earlier verbal conventions that safeguarded dignity and good taste, like the "owl curtain" in tragedy, always lowered for things and subjects that exceeded the necessary decency. The dominance of the stage image achieved its culmination in the era of romanticism, together with the use of ever-more-complicated machinery. This was also the point at which the irregular genres confirmed their preponderance, including a new one—romantic tragedy.

To the degree that dramatic events still arose in the baroque era independently of autonomous time and space (the human actor was subordinated to the illusion of the theatrical image), in the nineteenth century the event began to decidedly predominate over its own time and space (in practice this meant that the theatrical character was brought

THE THEATRICAL BOX OF ILLUSION: A SPACE FOR VISUALIZATION

into the foreground and endowed with the autonomous function of shaping time and space).

Dobrochna Ratajczak wrote that:

> "Thanks to this move, the veracity of the theatrical image, as revealed in the truth of its overall expression, began to depend to an increasingly strong degree on the 'socialization' and 'psychization' of space, on its semanticization, dependent in its form and character on the experiences, dreams, and moods, and the guilt and errors of the characters: what was individual, and also what was collective, social, and national, suddenly made a very distinct imprint on what had previously been absolute and abstract."[54]

It was at this time that the process of closing the space of the stage from the direction of the audience—or more strictly speaking, visual impact—reached its culmination. This was the point at which the principle of the ramp, or the boundary between the stage and the audience, was fixed. It is precisely this box model from the late nineteenth century that contemporary semiotics attempts to describe by constructing, as Juri Lotman does, oppositions of the type visible/invisible or existent/nonexistent[55] characterizing the fundamentals of the art of acting and the rules for making present a world built of signs, communiques, and signals.

The later domination of so-called irregular genres aiming at the spectacular tended to obscure the rhetorical tradition at the roots of modern theater. This rhetorical tradition was based on the art of dialogue and the craft of creating action and characters. This was not only the Aristotelian tradition inseparably linked with the category of *mimesis*, or the Platonic "perfect imitation," but also the tradition that attempted in modern times to define the "essence of the dramatic," to capture the basis of dramatic techniques, and finally to build up what was at first only a normative, theoretical model of the "ideal" drama, which later became perhaps overly descriptive.

This idealization of modern dramatic form, from the Renaissance to late Romanticism, was crowned by the model of the "absolute" drama invented by Peter Szondi for the contrastive description of the

---

[54] D. Ratajczak, *Przestrzeń w dramacie...*, 58.
[55] J. M. Lotman, *Semiotyka sceny*, "Teatr" 1 (1980), 89–99.

The rhetorical model: Freytag's pyramid

epic tendencies in dramaturgy that Szondi observed from the 1880s through the Second World War.[56] Szondi's absolute drama, defined as always present interpersonal events, blurred the historical polarity of the development of the regular and irregular genres. It also fostered the illusion that the influence of Cartesian dualism on dramatic construction and the subjectivization of theatrical space had become apparent late, only at the end of the nineteenth century.

Yet that model, oversimplifying the past, undoubtedly made it possible to grasp the essence of the changes in drama at the turn of the nineteenth and twentieth centuries when there did indeed take place a shift away from "pure relatedness" in the direction of "re-creating the interpersonal dialectic," and the negation of the being-present of interpersonal affairs and the opposition of subject and object was accompanied by the relativization of three "ideal" factors in dramatic form:

1. the present—through the past (Ibsen) or memories (Chekhov);
2. the interpersonal sphere—through the subjective perspective (Strindberg);
3. event-driven—through objective relations that the drama is intended to present (Hauptmann).

In what was already a period of the clear dialectical "epicization" of dramatic form, as evident in the most outstanding stage productions of the time, Gustav Freytag's "pure" theory of dramatic technique enjoyed special popularity, perhaps as a reaction against the changes underway.[57] Published for the first time in Germany in 1863, translated into many languages (into English in 1894) and repeatedly reprinted, it "served well into the twentieth century as the standard manual for young playwrights."[58]

Even now this theory is frequently treated as a catalogue of universal dramaturgical stratagems.[59] Although he drew his examples from the greats, from Sophocles, Shakespeare, Lessing, Goethe and Schiller, Freytag was seeking not so much the specifics of the dramatic masterpiece as "the fundamental laws of dramatic construction."[60] This is surely why

---

[56] P. Szondi, *Theory of the Modern Drama*, ed. and trans. M. Hays, Cambridge 1987.
[57] G. Freytag, *Die Technik des Dramas*, Darmstadt 1965.
[58] M. Carlson, *Theories of the Theatre*, 258–259.
[59] See G. Müller, *Dramaturgie des Theaters, des Horspiels und des Films*, Würzburg 1954.
[60] G. Freytag, *Die Technik des Dramas*, 7.

Freytag's Technique of the Drama[61] certainly served rather the ongoing output of "well-made plays" than the opening of new perspectives in the development of dramatic form.

According to Freytag, the essence of dramatic style is the making visible of the plot and interesting the audience mainly in its unfolding (this is a matter of the illusion of making-present in the present moment, as Henri Gouhier would say a hundred years later[62]). The plot itself would have to be subject to the rules of gradation and development (by showing the desire of the protagonist to struggle against adversity). It must also—no ifs, ands, or buts—lead up to the characteristic turning point that reveals the contradiction between intention and outcome (the principle of the turning point applies not only to tragedy, just before the ineluctable fulfillment of the verdict of Fate, but to an equal degree to comedy, of which both Molière and Sardou were always aware).

Freytag went on to state that the directly presented—revealed—plot (or the "essence of dramatic poetry") has three characteristics:
1. gradual development;
2. contrast (more precisely: this is a matter of the art of plot with the aid of contrasts, for instance of a pair of protagonists);
3. concentration (or placing emphasis on only moments of the action and characters; as is known, a tight construction brings the drama closer to the short story).

These remarks were accompanied by a postulated parallel development of the plot and the characters, in recognition of their mutual interdependence within the framework of yet another geometrical model: the so-called "dramatic line," with a clear direction and clear turning points. Characters are the source of action, Freytag states—both the actions and the words of the *personae* should be in accordance with their internal natures: it is the nature of the hero that explains his deeds, while making the plot seem necessary. On the other hand, however, plot must determine character, or define it. It is plot that places the protagonists in various situations, and we learn about their nature from the way they behave.

---

[61] G. Freytag, *Freytag's Techinique of the Drama: An Exposition and Art*, trans. and ed. E. J. MacEwan, Chicago 1894.

[62] H. Gouhier, *L'Essence du théâtre*, Paris 1968, 15–20.

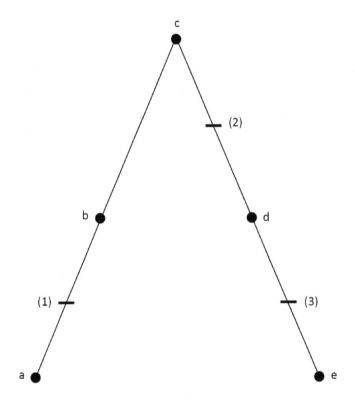

Figure 3. G. Freytag: The Pyramidal Structure of the Dramatic Model

THE THEATRICAL BOX OF ILLUSION: A SPACE FOR VISUALIZATION

As to the question of which is more important, character or plot, Aristotle came down unequivocally on the side of action plot. Freytag solved the problem in the following way: He distinguished two types of drama—Germanic and Romance. He credited the Germanic poets with greater aptitude in portraying character (the states and deeds of the protagonists are said to be shown "in a series of half-epic, half-lyrical images)." He held that the Romance poets, by contrast, were better at managing the action plot, which bore fruit in the "battles of words" that could take place without a change of place. In this dualistic view, Freytag's greatest exemplar of the Germanic drama was, of course, Shakespeare!

Freytag's theory involved the actual weakening of the traditional tension between the line of the development of character and the line of the development of the plot. This resulted from the conviction that the making present of the plot militates for the necessity of simultaneously displaying both the "external mask" of the characters, and the characters' hidden intentions (as facilitated by the conventions of monologues and asides). Freytag himself explained this principle of the rhetoric of drama as having to do with

> "the inner processes which man experiences from the first glow of perception to passionate desire and action, as well as the influences which one's own and others' deeds exert upon the soul; also the rushing forth of will power from the depths of man's soul toward the external world, and the influx of fashioning influences from the outer world into man's inmost being; also the coming into being of a deed, and its consequences on the human soul."[63]

Freytag, however, was not content with theoretically sanctioning the Cartesian "two theaters"; more significant, of course, was his conception of the "pyramidal structure" of the dramatic model, made up of five parts and three "crises" ("important theatrical actions"). Those parts are (a) the introduction; (b) the rising movement; (c) the climax; (d) the falling movement or return; and (e) the catastrophe. Parts (a) and (b) make up the first half of the plot, or the rising action, while parts (d) and (e) are the second half of the plot—the falling action.

The two halves of the plot are joined at part (c), the climax (which gives the line of action its pyramidal shape).

---

[63] G. Freytag, *Freytag's Technique...*, 18.

Each of the five parts is at the same time divided and joined together by the three crises, or important theatrical actions:
1. the rousing moment, which marks the initiation of the plot (between [a] the introduction and [b] the rising movement)
2. the tragic moment—the initiation of the counterplot (between [c] the climax and [d] the falling movement or return);
3. the moment of final tension, (which once again arises between [d] the falling movement or return and [e] the catastrophe)

Once again, it would seem, the ideally symmetrical model (where the culminating point [c] precisely bisects the line of the plot into two two-part segments: the rising [a-b-c] and falling [c-d-e]) conceals a principle of asymmetry. The rising part of the action contains only one moment of "crisis," the rousing moment (between [a] and [b]), while two such moments, the "tragic" moment (between [c] and [d]) and the moment of "the final tension" (between [d] and [e]), inevitably appear in the falling part of the action, after the culminating point. As a result of this, the geometrical pattern of action built into the modern model of the Italian stage was closer to the asymmetrical nature of the actor, the main vehicle of the plot, than to the spatial symmetry of perspective which had initially seemed to dominate both the actor and the plot.

MATHEMATICAL UNIVERSE

Modern theater was thus formed parallel to the development of changing dramatic conventions in the sixteenth to nineteenth centuries as a spatial art of depiction. The visual theatrical presentation, the actor's creation of character as an expression of the language of the body, and the line of plot were all depicted according to symmetrical or asymmetrical rules of geometry.

The abstract square image of the stage (a cube in its spatial version), inscribed with lines of central perspective, created the illusion of an infinite, unchanging, homogeneous space, and thus permitted the spectator "to take in the whole range of the stage with a single glance."[64] But an equal role in the creation of the stage image was played by the illusions produced by scenographic conventions and, increasingly importantly, the peopling of the stage with the motor forces embodied in human beings—the actors.[65] This is how, in the wake of the stereoscopic visual principle, modern individualism and a hierarchical conception of human existence entered the theater.[66]

The circle (sphere) of the actor's "speaking gestures" (with meaning inhering in each line of movement of every significant part of the body) was—regardless of the value of the Delsartian codification—an expression of the modern faith in the universality of the extra-linguistic emotional code, and also of the ubiquity of the "reading in" of intention that defined

---

[64] A. Hauser, *The Social History...*, 9.
[65] R. Arnheim, *Art and Visual Perception...*, 381.
[66] Ibid., 294–295.

each interpersonal relation (which according to contemporary psychology justifies the application of the theatrical metaphor in social life).[67]

This was also a new understanding of acting, not only as the art of declamation or singing, but as the artistic repletion of the space of the stage with a dynamic, three-dimensional image of the body in motion—a visual work of art constructed by the actor or dancer. And finally, the circle of gestures can be read as the taking up anew of the concept of Vitruvian man—in the Christian version disseminated in the Renaissance, when "the Vitruvian figure inscribed in a square and a circle became a symbol of the mathematical sympathy between microcosm and macrocosm."[68] Deserving of special treatment is the question, passed over here, of modern theater architecture, which was influenced alongside the Vitruvian tradition by Renaissance study of mnemonics and hermetism.[69]

The triangle of action (Freytag's Pyramid)—with its inscribed nexes of action—had, since the time of Sophocles, defined the linguistic development of the dramatic conventions. But only the transformation of drama on the box stage would elevate that geometrical model to the status of an obligatory rule of artisanal correctness. According to Zbigniew Raszewski it was precisely this model, in the sublimated version patterned on the crystal known as the bisphenoid—that constituted in general the essence of theatricality, making it possible to distinguish the dramatic/theatrical work from the epic or the lyric. Similar models, such as the triangle or the pyramid, were used to describe the dramatic structure, for example in the second half of the twentieth century by Richard Schechner.[70]

It seems that the pyramid of action, although discovered much earlier, was also used universally on the Italian stage. One of the distinguishing marks of this modern discovery was the serial principle. The pyramid of action became the temporal counterpart of the visual pyramid from

---

[67] See E. Burns, *Theatricality: A Study of Convention in the Theatre and in Social Life*, New York 1973, 8–21.
[68] R. Wittkower, *Architektural Principles in the Age of Humanism*, London 1949, 15.
[69] See F. A. Yates, *The Art of Memory*.
[70] Z. Raszewski, *Teatr w świecie widowisk*, Warszawa 1991, 161–170; R. Schechner, *Performance Theory*, New York and London 1988, 16–17.

Leonardo da Vinci's notebooks, which was inscribed in the box stage.[71] The ubiquity of the pyramid of action not only in tragedy (where it is a distinguishing trait of the genre) but also in modern comedy, and also in irregular or downright popular genres, including those that were mediated, results as well from the spatial (and not the temporal) structure of memory: "In perceiving an incident," Arnheim wrote, "during a happening we witness an organized sequence in which phases follow one another in a meaningful one-dimensional order. When the event is disorganized or incomprehensible . . . no time bond connects these momentary phases, because time by itself can create succession, but not order"[72].

---

[71] See D. Thomas, *Embodied Phenomenology*, "Journal of Literary Semantics" 42 (1) (January 2013).

[72] R. Arnheim, *Art and Visual Perception...*, 375.

THE DREAMS
OF "INHIBITED PRACTITIONERS"

THE IDEAL WORK OF THE NEW THEATER: APPIA'S MODEL

An unusual conjunction of three tendencies then prominent in European theatrical thinking and practice determined the formulation of the idea of the New Theater at the turn of the 19th and 20th centuries. First, to capture and name the essence of theater, second, to give the theatrical performance the status of a work of art, and third, to create a separate and distinct art, the art of theater, out of various materials. Each of these tendencies, the essential, the aesthetic and the autonomous, contributed to the irrevocable transformation of theatrical style within the box stage.

But the postulated New Theater did not result from aspirations so homogeneous as they are frequently depicted. Aside from the accepted autonomy (or separateness) of the theatrical work among other arts, and also the perpetuation of the idea of the synthetic nature of the theatrical spectacle, the remaining postulates in the area of directing, stage design, and acting, the prerogatives of the artist of the theater, the hierarchy of variously defined ingredients were already of a derivative and heterogeneous nature. Perhaps for this reason the seekers of a New Theater: Edward Gordon Craig, Adolphe Appia, Antonin Artaud, for various reasons frequently chose the path of aesthetic manifestos over firsthand theatrical experience. They have even been referred to as "inhibited practitioners."[73] But perhaps more important, it turned out, were problems with the creation of such a universal model of the theatrical work, in the form (despite everything) of the Italian box and its conventions, which enjoyed popularity over several centuries.

---

[73] See D. Bablet, *La mise en scène contemporaine. 1, 1887–1914*, Paris 1968.

From the perspective of time, it is increasingly easy to discern a polarity in the New Theater. This was most elegantly expressed by one of the participants in the movement, the "great eclectic," Max Reinhardt. He formulated two opposed solutions: either "truth against convention" or "style against realism."[74] This formula can serve as a motto not only for the polemics of the naturalists and the symbolists from the late nineteenth century, but also, apparently with equal insight, for the whole of twentieth-century theater, which in various ways departed from the absolutization of the theatrical world in the place of pure interpersonal relations, introducing, in Peter Szondi's formula, "the inexpressible as well as the expressed, what was hidden in the soul as well as the idea already alienated from its subject."[75]

Jan Błoński wrote in his introduction to the Polish version of J. L. Styan's *Modern Drama in Theory and Practice*: "The naturalistic trend (dramaturgy as well) was never again to be extinguished and in fact accompanies to this day literary creativity apparently based—although not always loudly—on the *basso continuo*. Similarly, the countercurrent, although it takes on ever-new forms (monumental, ritual, magical theater)—is very distant from the primal assumptions of symbolism. Announced by two great precursors, Wagner and Ibsen, the bipolar nature of the theatrical sensitivity was thereby perpetuated and nothing indicates that it will burn out a century and a half later."[76]

Things were similar, after all, in the era of the counterculture of the 1960s and 1970s, when on the one hand there was a futile effort to revive the connection between theater and ritual and the return to the myth of the "ideal community" was proclaimed. On the other hand, there was confinement to the circle of the theatricality of everyday life and its unmasking. There was a search for the human "primal substance" (Grotowski, The Living Theater) or people were shown as "the eternal actor" (the productions of The Bread and Puppet Theater, the Strehlerian revivals of *commedia dell'arte*).

---

[74] B. Crémieux, *Conversation sur le théâtre (...) avec Max Reinhardt*, "Je suis partout" (28 X 1933).

[75] P. Szondi, *Theory of the Modern Drama*, 7.

[76] J. Błoński, *Przedmowa*, in: J. L. Styan, *Współczesny dramat w teorii i scenicznej praktyce*, trans. M. Sugiera, Wrocław 1995, 10.

Embedded at the sources of the twentieth-century theater, therefore, was naturalistic-symbolic synchrony, as theater's answer to phenomena existing earlier or in parallel in literature[77] (the symbolism of the turn of the nineteenth and twentieth centuries was not a straightforward reaction to naturalism; both tendencies coexisted, mutually complementing and defining each other). Both the naturalists and the symbolists pointed out the specificity of the art of the theater. The naturalists started with the assumption that only in the theater was it possible to repeat real reality and make visible the decisive influence of the surroundings of people (as Denis Bablet wrote, "in this way they mistook the subject with its image, life with its presentation, and they replaced the image of reality"[78]). The symbolists in turn believed that it was precisely the visual-aural spectacle that supported (and fulfilled) the efforts of poetry or painting to express the "essence of things," to penetrate to the "*deep*-seated self" of man and the order of the world that evaded consciousness. Both of them perpetuated the idea of the synthetic nature of the new, integrated (to speak in the language of today) work of theatrical art.

In the theater, the greatest difference between the symbolists and the naturalists had to do with their contrasting understanding of the ends of art, and also of the relationship between art and reality. They also had different solutions to the issue of the choice and hierarchy of components in the of the new theatrical work. According to André Antoine, naturalistic literature would ensure the rebirth of the theater, and the starting point for stage design would be the replication of the setting of the plot (the postulate of "real" decoration). In stagings of the classics, reliant upon other dramatic conventions, there was an attempt to preserve local color through the use of historical reconstruction.

In Antoine's theater, the actor was to be a "simple instrument in the hands of the poet and the stage manager."[79] The secondary status of the theatrical creation in relation to literature resulted from the fact that the physical person of the actor is only a part of the acting character. After re-creating the setting of the plot, the stage manager established

---

[77] See K. Wyka, *Modernizm polski*, Kraków 1968, 38, 115.
[78] D. Bablet, *La mise en scène contemporaine...*
[79] *Conférence faite par M. Antoine au Théâtre de l'Odeon*, "Courrier de La Plata" (17 VIII 1903).

the movements of the actors (regarded as the most intensive means of expression), the placement of characters, and the interpretation and tempo of the dialogue (the latter was one of the non-material actions of direction). The slogan that the stage was "a faithful copy of reality without selection or synthesis"[80] (in the theater—world relation) coexisted for Antoine with the criterion of the unity of the stage vision (and therefore, however, the synthesis—within the theatrical work—of the following components: literature, the re-created setting, actors concealed behind the acting characters).

The later work of the greatest theatrical realist, Konstantin Stanislavski, transcended this formulation of the program of naturalism, but in the first period of the Moscow Art Theater (MAT, 1898–1905)—which he himself called "external realism"—the Russian in fact repeated Antoine's assumptions. Although he had a different conception of the vocation of actor from the beginning ("the one king and ruler of the stage"[81]), his theater continued to acknowledge the dominance of literature, and the whole so-called Stanislavski System or Method, based on conscious technique and a creative process of experience, relied on a multi-stage reconciliation of the psychological truth of the character with the internal truth of the actor. This was therefore also a matter of creating a synthesis of literature and theater. With one important difference: for Antoine, it was the stage director who was supposed to perform the synthesis, while for Stanislavski things were to be decided collectively by the whole group.

The symbolists took a different view of the problem of the autonomy of the theater and the relation of literature, performance, and reality. Rejecting naturalistic imitation, they placed the accent on the significance of the co-creative imagination. One of their postulates was trust in the poetic word, recited against the background of anti-illusionist, painterly decorations. Another was the search for new forms of the art of suggestion and evocation that acted simultaneously on all the beholder's senses. Creator of the Paris Théâtre d'Art (1890–1893), Paul Fort developed the idea of synthesis in the first pronouncement in favor of the total theater: "the orchestration of words, music, colors, and smell." He dreamed of

---

[80] D. Bablet, *La mise en scène contemporaine*…
[81] C. Stanislavsky, *My Life in Art*, London 1924, 543.

a theater of "pure vision, with no text or actors."[82] Another participant in the symbolist reaction, Aurélien Lugné-Poe, founder of the Théâtre de l'Œuvre in Paris (1893–1912), formulated the slogan of "abstract acting and dehumanized playing for the sake of playing," the disintegration of the theater and a return to the roots.[83] This foreshadowed the second phase of the projected reform, associated with the names of Appia and Craig.

In the first phase of the New Theater quest at the end of the nineteenth century, the phase of naturalistic-symbolic synchronism, there was a marked tendency that was proper to the whole cycle of theatrical revolution: from synthesis, the annexation of other arts and external reality (following the principle of unity), to the elimination and questioning of literature, the context of reality (the postulates of the symbolists), and next the actor (as anticipated by Lugné-Poe, in the formula of the "Übermarionette" conceived of by Craig), painting (as done by Appia), and finally the whole received theater.

Plans for such thorough elimination, and dreams of "pure" theater created anew appeared as a reaction to the unresolved dispute between the naturalists and symbolists. In the second phase of the New Theater quest (the negation of the existing theatrical style and the program of a "return to roots"), especially in Craig's thinking, the opposition between the illusion of representation and the effective power of the imagination took on the form of a modernist contradiction of life and death. Founder and editor of a magazine promoting theater reform: "The Mask" (1908–1929), Edward Gordon Craig wrote about the aspiration of the "Übermarionette" that replaced the actor to "aim to clothe itself with a death-like Beauty while exhaling a living spirit."[84] On the side of life, Craig saw nature, unfit to become a model, and all the more material for art. On the side of death he placed imagination—the proper source of creation. But he was more than just another symbolist. He demanded something new—namely the construction anew of the structure of the work of the art of the theater. He rejected not only the idea of synthesis, but also its compromise expression, relying on the inclusion of other

---

[82] D. Bablet, *La mise en scène contemporaine…*
[83] Ibid.
[84] E. G. Craig, *The Actor and the Über-marionette*, "The Mask" 1 (2) (April 1908), 12.

arts—literature, music, the visual arts—in a new aesthetic quality (similar to the way the avant-garde painters saw things, experimenting within the circle of their "-isms" with the material of the theater[85]).

Craig treated the idea of the autonomy of the theater in a maximalist way. He dreamed of reaching back to the mythical sources, to the ideal state before contamination by foreign influences and dependence. The way to the theatrical Arcadia was to be through the dancing "Übermarionette," subordinated, as in a Far-Eastern trance—to the will of the one priest of the New Art: the Artist of the Theater. Indeed, the proper constituents of the theater proposed by Craig: "action, words, line, colour, rhythm"[86]—were simply other names for the traditional components of theatrical art: the person-actor, literature, the spatiality, and temporality of the performance. Reform would thus consist of not so much a change of materials, as the construction of a perfect aesthetic object, a repeatable and therefore lasting work of visual art, fitting completely into the received box stage.

Inspired by Wagner's thought, the Swiss theater theorist and set designer, Adolphe Appia, went farther: namely, he desired to construct a model of the theatrical work according to an unambiguously set hierarchy of materials. Among the seekers of the New Theater at the turn of the nineteenth and twentieth centuries (who for various reasons usually preferred aesthetic manifestos to real-life work in the theater), only Appia bequeathed to the future a logical vision of the autonomous theatrical work, the only concrete and precisely defined model that found acknowledgment in those times. In his book *La mise en scéne du théâtre Wagnerien*, published in Paris in 1895, he defined the character of such a work, named its ingredients, and included it in a hierarchical structure.

Furthermore, Appia's model expresses the antinomy of the New Theater quest: it unites the postulate of the truth of expression (the poet-musician as the constructor of the whole; the actor-dancer and singer as the king of an empty, rhythmic space) and the style of theatrical form, permanent thanks to the basing of the theatrical work on a musical structure:

---

[85] See R. L. Goldberg, *Performance: Live Art 1909 to the Present*, London 1979; J. G. Glover, *The Cubist Theatre*, Michigan 1980; M. Kirby, *Futurist Performance*, New York 1986.

[86] E. G. Craig, *On the Art of the Theater*, London 1911, 188.

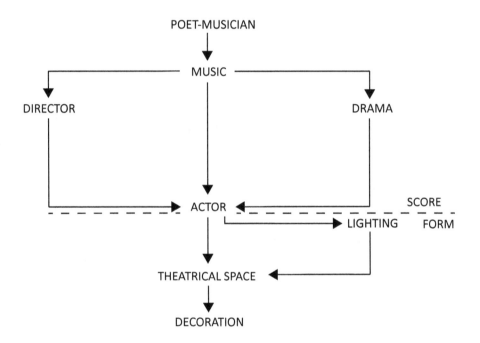

Figure 4. Appia's *Worttondrama* model

> "In terms of scenic representation music is *Time* ... music shapes a whole set of dimensions: first of all the sequence of choreographic units, then crowd movements right down to individual gestures, and finally, with more or less insistence, the proportions of the inanimate scene."[87]

Appia stated that the musical "partitura" (score) of the *Worttondrama* offers a chance for the complete designing of the theatrical performance, freed from the dictates of accident, subordinated fully to the one artist of the theater: the Poet-Musician.

Only music, in Appia's opinion, can fully define the course and shape of the performance—designating time and space (through the strictness of proportions), and also the movement of the actor. Drama of the Wagnerian type, as opposed to spoken drama and to the ossified opera, was defined by Appia as inscribed in the dramatic form of a new variety of persistence: the persistence of the internal drama, having nothing in common with the "external drama of life." The soul of this new type of drama would, according to him, be music:

> "What characterizes Wagnerian drama and constitutes its high value, is the power of possesses, by its music, to *express* the interior drama, whereas spoken drama can mer[e]ly *signify* it. As music is *Time*, it gives to the interior drama a duration that must correspond to the length of the performance itself. ... Wagnerian drama is quite distinctly set apart from spoken drama, for it does not draw its measure in time from everyday life, but creates a duration of its own."[88]

Appia based his hierarchy of the elements of the play on two types of relations of dependence: designation and intermediation. Each element either "designated" the ingredient to follow, or exercised an intermediary function between other elements of the play.

At the very top of these hierarchical associations stands the "Poet-Musician" (*à la* Wagner) as the "most powerful of artists," creating Time and Space and subordinating to himself the elements of theatrical technique. In this sense, the personality of the Poet-Musician forms the play and suffuses all its elements through the intermediation of the most important of them, the music.

---

[87] A. Appia, *Staging Wagnerian Drama*, trans. P. Loeffler, Basel 1982, 40.
[88] Ibid., 41, 45.

The ideal work of the New Theater: Appia's model

It is precisely music that establishes the remaining ingredients according to the needs of dramatic expression, that "is the soul of drama," expressing the interior drama, and from the point of view of the performance is Time: it defines the choreographic and dramatic image. Music designates directly the three ingredients of the dramatic work: the above-mentioned interior drama of the Wagnerian type, next the principle of staging, identified with the recreative role of the stage manager, and finally the actor—understood as a "bearer of the role," deprived of individuality: "the actor's role lives by the measures supplied by the music."[89]

In Appia's view, the director is not an autonomous artist. He rather appears as a despotic coach in service to the Poet-Musician. This despot is to watch over the strict ordering of forms of expression (shapes, lights, colors) in the name of the artist, giving the music the proper form and strength and, through its intermediation, shattering the audience's inertia and subordinating the audience to the play: "Any director dealing with Wagner's work must thus let himself be guided exclusively and with all humility by what is revealed to him through the drama's true life."[90]

But the actor remains in the center of the structure thus envisioned, the representative of the only reality worthy of the theater: the "reality of the human body." Music designates the actor's role for him, as well as "the sequence of choreographic units"[91] or the movement, directly. The actor, in turn, intermediates: between the staging and the decorative form as well as between the play and the theatrical space (n.b. in Appia's scenographic designs, there are no images of the human body).

"The drama," wrote Appia, "can only determine staging if it uses the actor as its intermediary."[92] The privileged position of the actor results precisely from the fact that he is the intermediary between the *partitura* and the form of the presentation. His "role" is on the side of the *partitura*, together with the music, the drama, and the staging. His body remains on the other side at the same time: the form made present.

But the actor pays a high price for this double presence: the price of renunciation "of his whole being, in order to become strictly *musical*."

---

[89] Ibid., 53.
[90] Ibid., 47.
[91] Ibid., 40.
[92] Ibid., 53.

THE DREAMS OF "INHIBITED PRACTITIONERS"

The actor must also resign from "not only his personality, but every *right* to his role as well. The more complete his renunciation, the better the actor has fulfilled his task."[93]

Nevertheless it is the body of the actor—the real "vehicle of the role"—that should dominate over form, composed (aside from the actor) of the theatrical space, lighting, and decoration. The actor, in turn, mediates: between the staging and the decorative form as well as between the play and "the spatial arrangement, which in turn is shaped by the actor, or rather by the impulses coming from his role."[94] "With regards to the actor, scene painting is entirely subordinated to lighting and the spatial arrangements."[95]

The decoration itself occupies a lower place in this hierarchy. Its painted variant is "the least important element" of all the elements of the production—as the main vehicle for the illusory "lifeless signs" that are necessary for the staging of traditional drama based on the external appearances of life.

> "The means to achieve a fusion between actor and scenic environment did not exist before the advent of Wagnerian drama," wrote Appia. "Staging concerned itself with innumerable details, which, adding one to the other, were supposed to create the necessary suggestion. As the poet could not *express* the interior drama, he was forced to simply *indicate* it by scenic action; play and performance were thus, in their own way, adequate: both were incapable of expressing *essence*, were forced to merely indicate it, the play by mirroring the surface of life, the performance by a use of lifeless signs."[96]

In the first three-dimensional theatrical spatial designs for the works of Wagner that he created at the same time, Appia not only demolished the perspective system and rear-stage decorations that were still in force. With extraordinary boldness, he also undermined the very principles of the symmetry and homogeneity of the theatrical image. He did exactly the opposite of what all his predecessors had done as decorators of the Italian stage: instead of subordinating the acting to the principles of spatial symmetry and the ubiquitous signification, he decided to make

---

[93] Ibid., 57, 55.
[94] Ibid., 54.
[95] Ibid., 50.
[96] Ibid., 51.

precisely space asymmetrical and ambiguous, in an analogy to the natural principles of expression proper to the actor and the lighting.

Asymmetrical space thus intermediates between lighting and painted decorations[97]—only in this indirect manner is it possible to reconcile the natural contradiction resulting from illuminated, flat canvas. Active lighting, on the other hand, enters between the actor and space and decoration; thanks to this intermediating function it becomes the most important element in the "theatrical revolution" propagated by Appia:

> "Lighting constitutes the most important element of fusion by relating the actor to both spatial arrangements and scene painting. What we may thus lose quantitatively in terms of *sign* (painting) is gained by a direct expression of life."[98]

From a later perspective it has been acknowledged that Appia's greatest contribution was precisely the reform of lighting—not only the replacement of painted stage decorations with new "light" decorations, but also the application of the expressive function of light[99] (Appia intended to use light as "visual music").

With special acuity, Appia expressed the revelation by electrical lighting (introduced to the theater on a wide scale in the 1880s) of the contrast between the three-dimensional body of the moving actor and the pseudo-illusion of flat, dead canvas pretending to be interiors and landscapes (electricity lit the space of the stage far more brightly than the diffuse light of gas lamps).

In his search for a way out of this contradiction, Appia initiated the replacement of those painterly decorations by three-dimensional asymmetric architectonic compositions. This would become universal in the following years. This created the conditions for emphasizing the aesthetic values of the human body in motion, the body creating a new type of spatial relations in the theater (which was aided by the manipulation of electrical lighting—moving and variable). Attention was especially attracted by the rhythmic spaces projects that arose to "accentuate the human body to musical accompaniment" in cooperation

---

[97] Ibid., 50.
[98] Ibid., 54.
[99] Z. Raszewski, *Wstęp*, in: A. Appia, *Żywa sztuka czy martwa natura?...*, "Pamiętnik Teatralny" 4 (1956), 586.

with the inventor of rhythmics, Émile Jaques-Dalcroze, to whom Appia wrote in May 1906, "the life of the body tends towards anarchy and therefore towards grossness. It is music which can liberate it by imposing its discipline upon it."[100]

In his later works (*L'Oeuvre d'art vivant*—1919; *Art Vivant? ou nature morte?*—1922), Appia renounces the temptation of perfecting his model of the ideal work of art of the New Theater. Over time he distanced himself from his own revolutionary aesthetic ideas, rejecting not only traditional stage design, but also the theatrical building, in favor of portraying life in a not-fully-defined space and time, with an active part played by the audience, whether on the musical side, or in the action.

From the historical perspective the more interesting thing seems to be not that final enunciation of the "theater-holiday" (Grotowski's "the day that is holy"[101]) to which the theatrical communitarians of the 1960s and 1970s link themselves, but rather Appia's initial vision—the theoretics of the asymmetrical structure of the theater, derived from the spirit of Wagnerian dissonant musical harmony.

---

[100] Appia to Dalcroze, May 1906, in: *Frameworks, Artworks, Place: The Space of Perception in the Modern World*, ed. T. Mehigan, Amsterdam 2008, 125.

[101] See J. Grotowski, *Holiday (Święto): The Day That Is Holy*, in: *The Grotowski Sourcebook*, ed. R. Schechner, L. W. Wylam, London 1997.

THE LEGACY OF SYMBOLISM: ARTAUD'S MAGICAL MODEL

Both the naturalists and the symbolists wanted a theater that expressed "the truth," as opposed to the received stage conventions. They had, however, different conceptions of both truth and convention. The former dreamed of the truth of objective knowledge, turning to the reality of the milieu and the characters it defined (consenting to the mediation of literature and the living actor). The latter opted for the truth of the experience of non-mimetic art. Aiming for the absolute, the expression of the inexpressible, they chose evocation instead of showing (they saw in naturalism, after all, just another illusionistic convention) and dreamed at times of removing the actor (and literature) from the theater.

The whole search for the New Theater began at the end of the nineteenth century with the questioning of the actor's domination of the theater. This beginning is sometimes forgotten, with the accent often being placed instead on the tendency—derived from the ideas and practices of Wagner (*Gesamtkunstwerk*)—toward synthesizing the theatrical art and making it autonomous, while at the same time transforming the theatrical space (where, after the electricity revolution and the spread of Adolphe Appia's ideas, came the "death of the *praktikabel*[102] conquered by the platform,"[103] and after that the wide acceptance of the idea of "empty space"). After all, the search for the New Theater gave birth to the revolt against the nineteenth-century star system that was based on the rhetoric of declamation and the "semiotics" of gesture.

---

[102] Praktikabel: structural elements for stages, traditionally made of wood.
[103] Z. Raszewski, *Krótka historia teatru polskiego*, Warszawa 1977, 205.

THE DREAMS OF "INHIBITED PRACTITIONERS"

New Theater theorists decided to downgrade actors and subordinate them to the overriding idea of the spectacle. In their opinion, star actors—using their skills at making an immediate impact—made it impossible for the performance/spectacle to achieve its most important aesthetic aims by transforming the play into a separate, autonomous, and synthetic (based on the synthesis of the arts) work of art. This overriding idea—guaranteeing the unity of the work of theatrical art—was first sought in literature (the search for the New Theater was, after all, kicked off by two revolutions in dramaturgy: naturalism and symbolism) or in the function of the Theater Artist, who assumed responsibility for the entirety of the work—this is what Craig, Appia, and Wyspiański thought.

It was Antonin Artaud, co-creator of the Parisian Le Théâtre Alfred Jarry (1926–1929), ideologue of The Theater of Cruelty, who wrote most unsettlingly about the new acting:

> "The actor is both an element of first importance, since it is upon the effectiveness of his work that the success of the spectacle depends, and a kind of passive and neutral element, since he is rigorously denied all personal initiative. It is a domain in which there is no precise rule."[104]

Artaud was regarded as one of the most outstanding theatrical symbolists of the twentieth century. J. L. Styan, clearly no admirer of Artaud's, wrote that

> "while in this century Wagner's seminal thinking has ruggedly supported one theatrical experiment after another . . . the great originators in the symbolist vein—Pirandello, Artaud, Beckett, Genet—are very few, and of these there are only one or two to whom the stage repeatedly returns for a basic design."

Styan went on to add rather dismissively that

> "The symbolist and ritual theater is strong in our heritage, and doubtless it would be with us even without the exertions of an Artaud or a Peter Brook."[105]

It has also been written about Antonin Artaud that he was the most radical proponent of surrealism, and that he created a surrealistic version of the New Theater in the wake of the earlier naturalistic and symbolist variants. In terms of creating a surrealist theater, Artaud—with

---

[104] A. Artaud, *The Theater and Its Double*, trans. M. C. Richards, New York 1958, 98.
[105] J. L. Styan, *Modern Drama in Theory and Practice*, Vol. 2: *Symbolism, Surrealism and the Absurd*, Cambridge 1986, 183.

The legacy of symbolism: Artaud's magical model

similarities to the case of Appia—remained an "inhibited practitioner." Henri Béhar wrote that:

> "There was ... never any theater or any man of the theater who more or less regularly mounted surrealist plays, just as Antoine used to do with naturalistic plays, or Paul Fort and Lugné-Poe with symbolist plays. This role could only be fulfilled by the Alfred Jarry Theater, if it had not become the object of the tragic misunderstanding between its founders and the surrealist group."[106]

It was not only the failure of the Alfred Jarry Theater (which staged only four plays in the years 1927–1930), however, that defined Artaud's actual part in the quest for a New Theater. Although he repeated on multiple occasions the postulates of his great predecessors, Craig and Appia, he distanced himself the most from the understanding of the art of the theater as a game with convention or aesthetic contemplation:

> "The objective of Appia and Craig remains an objective of an aesthetic nature ... For them, the performance has become the ultimate boundary and the advent of a new art. They were the first who wanted the 're-theatralization of the theater,' and ... since 1924 that intention had seemed monstrous to Artaud. His goal was precisely of a spiritual nature, and he did not hesitate to call it mystical. The comparison with Appia and Craig made it possible to at least recall that fundamental idea that, for Artaud, there existed within the theater a particle that was connected with 'metaphysics.'"[107]

Artaud not only returned to the aesthetic or religious "roots" of performance. He created a theater that resurrected the therapeutic function of myths: a total theater full of "blood and terror," based on the maximization of effects and producing a trance in which both audience and actors participate. The magic of the Theater of Cruelty lay in the relations between spectator and actor, event and myth, and theater and cosmogony (the essential drama of creation).

With Artaud, the consistent rejection of the psychological theater that operates through words resulted from the condemnation of western rationalism and the delusion of understanding man and the world that it produced. "If confusion is the sign of the times," he wrote, "I see at

---

[106] H. Béhar, *Etude sur le théâtre dada et surréaliste*, Paris 1967.
[107] A. Virmaux, *Antonin Artaud et le théâtre*, Paris 1970, 135.

the root of this confusion a rupture between things and words, between things and the ideas and signs that are their representation."[108]

Artaud thus propounded the need for a return—in the sacral space of the theater—to the Pre-Christian Beginning of magical ritual that reconciled things and signs, the conscious and the subconscious, object and subject, individual and collective. The sense of these contradictions and the need to reconcile them were driven by an illness variously diagnosed by specialists as paraphrenia, what we now call schizoid personality disorder, or schizophrenia.[109] Artaud described this postulated therapeutic theater as if it were an analogy to mythical reality. The identity of the traits of the two phenomena is striking—from the elimination of the boundaries between the spheres of spirit and matter, being and thought, or life and death, to the concept of cyclical time, the intermingling of sense data with the productions of the mind, or total axiology, and so on.

Yet Artaud's intentions went beyond making the structure of myth present in the theater. He was more concerned with the effectiveness of the magical ritual into which the theater should be transformed, and restoring its status as a magical object evoking *surrealité*. One of Artaud's better known ideas was the comparison of the theater to the bubonic plague, interpreted as a necessary, periodic return of society to the world of "primal chaos," liquidating for a time any established social order and releasing the subconscious powers of criminality in order to make possible the magical rebirth of the world.

Jan Błoński, the Polish commentator on and translator of Artaud's work, insightfully grasped the problem connected with any attempt at an analysis or even a repetition of the Artaudian vision: "How to intellectually systematize a dream that—in its very assumptions—should remain beyond the compass of the intellect?"

In his systematic analysis of Artaud, Błoński showed that the keys to his poetics of the magical theater are the bywords "ritual anarchy" and "cruelty freely conceived."[110] In the first of these formulas, ritual

---

[108] A. Artaud, *The Theater and Its Double*, 7.
[109] See L. Kolankiewicz, *Święty Artaud*, Warszawa 1988, 59.
[110] J. Błoński, *Artaud i teatr magiczny*, in: A. Artaud, *Teatr i jego sobowtór*, trans. J. Błoński, Warszawa 1966, 17, 24, 25.

The legacy of symbolism: Artaud's magical model

means not so much the sacral as the need for a code—a guarantee of comprehensibility. Anarchy, on the other hand, is a particular kind of poetic basis and, at the same time, a "return to zero": the freeing of the theater from intellect, psychology, and society.

Ritual, however, is to be precisely the form that makes possible and at the same time liquidates anarchy understood in this way.

In the second formula, freedom clashes with the concept of cruelty, which is basic to Artaud's system. According to the notorious idea of the Theater of Cruelty (a title that the artist used for no fewer than two of his manifestos), it is a matter of rigor, ruthlessness, decisiveness, and the principle of bringing "all things to the ineluctable goal and termination, and at any cost." The described and felt ceremonies observed a poetics of the magical theater of their own, expressed most frequently through paradox and attempting to reconcile contradictions and opposites.

Yet this New Theater was more than a poetic vision. Artaud was one of the few Reformers who was able to see the fulfillment of his theatrical utopia. What is more, it was precisely Artaud—and he alone—who authenticated the call for "a return to the sources" and had a ready model that had been found, admittedly by accident, in reality.

This means, of course, the famous Balinese theater that appeared in Paris at the 1931 colonial exposition. It was precisely the dancers from the distant island who made possible an attempt at the literal liquidation of Artaud's mental contradictions. In an enthusiastic review,[111] Artaud described the Balinese dancers as the ideal of the dynamic accumulation of forms come true, taking on dramatic values in a variable, artistic, pulsating space that was additionally filled with sound:

> "This spectacle offers us a marvelous complex of pure stage images, for the comprehension of which a whole new language seems to have been invented: the actors with their costumes constitute veritable living, moving hieroglyphs. And these three-dimensional hieroglyphs are in turn brocaded with a certain number of gestures—mysterious signs which correspond to some unknown, fabulous, and obscure reality which we here in the Occident have completely repressed."[112]

---

[111] "La Nouvelle Revue Française" 10 (1931). Broadened version: A. Artaud, *On the Balinese Theater*, in: idem, *The Theater and Its Double*, trans. M. C. Richards, New York 1958, 53–67.

[112] Ibid., 61.

THE DREAMS OF "INHIBITED PRACTITIONERS"

For Artaud, the Balinese spectacle was an example of "pure intellectualism" based on a complex system of semi-ritual theatrical signs. It was the fulfillment of the magical and metaphysical theater: "pure and autonomous artistry"—"in the perspective of hallucination and fear."

> "The drama does not develop as a conflict of feelings but as a conflict of spiritual states, themselves ossified and transformed into gestures-diagrams. In a word, the Balinese have realized, with the utmost rigor, the idea of pure theater, where everything, conception and realization alike, has value, has existence only in proportion to its degree of objectification *on the stage*. They victoriously demonstrate the absolute preponderance of the director (*metteur en scene*) whose creative power *eliminates words*. The themes are vague, abstract, extremely general. They are given life only by the fertility and intricacy of all the artifices of the stage which impose upon our minds like the conception of a metaphysics derived from a new use of gesture and voice."[113]

Fascinating to Europeans, Balinese culture and civilization—characterized by fire and dance—had at its disposal exactly those things that were a dream, or at least a foreshadowing, for those looking for the New Theater a hundred years ago. A puppet depicted the spirit more fully than a living, thinking person (Balinese theater frequently represented spirits, not people).

> "These mechanically rolling eyes, pouting lips, and muscular spasms, all producing methodically calculated effects which forbid any recourse to spontaneous improvisation, these horizontally moving heads that seem to glide from one shoulder to the other as if on rollers, everything that might correspond to immediate psychological necessities, corresponds as well to a sort of spiritual architecture, created out of gesture and mime but also out of the evocative power of a system, the musical quality of a physical movement, the parallel and admirably fused harmony of a tone ... This purely popular and not sacred theater gives us an extraordinary idea of the intellectual level of a people who take the struggles of a soul preyed upon by ghosts and phantoms from the beyond as the basis for their civic festivals."[114]

The actor was thus born at the moment of entry into a religious trance, at the moment of the annihilation of his own self and the complete surrender to an alien spirit that became present in the uncontrolled movements of his own body.

---

[113] Ibid., 53–54.
[114] Ibid., 55–56.

"A kind of terror seizes us at the thought of these mechanized beings, whose joys and griefs seem not their own but at the service of age-old rites, as if they were dictated by superior intelligences. In the last analysis it is this impression of a superior and prescribed Life which strikes us most in this spectacle that so much resembles a rite one might profane."[115]

It is not exactly clear which kind of Balinese performance served as the basis for Artaud's poetical generalizations. It is known, however, that the encounter with this theater was of decisive significance in shaping Artaud's views, introducing a modicum of order into what Jan Błoński described as "a thicket of incredibly complicated relations among a variety of formal ranks and configurations that—at least at first glance—are dissonant, in reverse symmetry."[116]

This is why mutually exclusive guidelines accompany each other in a conflict-free way in the description of the Balinese theater:

"a dramatic but familiar subject"—"the themes are vague";

"these spiritual signs have a precise meaning"—"the metaphysics of natural disorder";

"greater emotional value of a certain number of perfectly learned and above all masterfully applied conventions"—"matter as revelation";

"mathematical meticulousness"—"lessons in spirituality";

"not sacred theater"—"something of the ceremonial quality of a religious rite";

"an innate sense of the absolute and magical symbolism of nature"—"things perform a strange about-face before becoming abstractions again."

A model of theatrical action composed of nine levels or spheres as a result of the resolution of these contradictions can be found in Artaud's profession-manifesto.

The arrangement of nine concentric circles is particularly apt here, as it illustrates not so much a scheme of hierarchical dependencies (as in Appia's model) as the coexistence of certain constantly violated planes, from the sphere of matter to the sphere of spirit, from chaos to ritual, from the concrete to abstraction.

---

[115] Ibid., 58.
[116] J. Błoński, *Artaud i teatr magiczny*, 28–29.

THE DREAMS OF "INHIBITED PRACTITIONERS"

The basis of the theatrical work is inscribed in the first sphere: the approach to metaphysical issues—the return to a "reality of matter, dreams, and myth"—and thus in the programmatic axioms liberated from intellect (things), psychology (dreams), and society (myth).

The next four spheres, from the second to the fifth, represent the material components of the performance.

First: "magical, living space"—a separate space common to the actors and audience, where the priest/*metteur-en-scene* is in charge of everything.

Next: sound ("unbearable and piercing") and signs: lighting, objects, actors, words.

Finally, ritual action—with all its dynamism.

Some doubts may arise over the privileging of sound over other varieties of signs. This is a matter, however, of emphasizing (in the footsteps of Artaud) the function of sound in initiation which, after the sacralization of the discrete space lays the ground for the spectacle proper, serving the induction of the actors, and also the audience, into a kind of trance.

In the realm of signs, it is worth noting the significant reversal of the hierarchy. In the European theater—rejected by Artaud—the actor's gesture (not to mention the subservient role of props and lighting) is fleshed out by the word. In the vision of the Theater from Bali the most important thing, according to Artaud, is the "physical," "concrete" language of the stage, dominated by the language of gestures (meaningful only in that ritual, magical space). Words appeared only in an objective, extra-conceptual function, as if before the birth of intellectual language.

The basic slogans of Artaud's program—the poetics of ritual anarchy (closely linked for example to the making present of myths in magical, living space), physical concreteness, "total speech," the maximization of effects (resulting from the role of sounds and other varieties of signs), and finally the magical unrepeatability of ritual—can be ascribed to the "material" spheres of the performance.

The sixth to the ninth spheres are the elements of the performance that already belong to the order of psychic phenomena (in his description of the Balinese theater, Artaud expressly mixed the elements that he actually perceived, for instance through the sense of hearing, with those that he wanted to perceive and, it inevitably seems, those formed in the psyches of all participants).

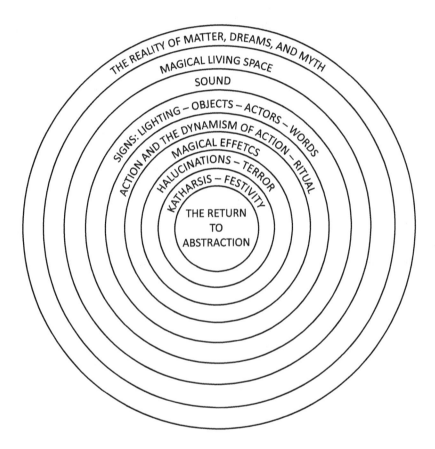

Figure 5. Artaud's Model of Theatrical Action

THE DREAMS OF "INHIBITED PRACTITIONERS"

And thus in turn: "magical effects," arising as a result of the rise of total theater as a result of the maximization of effects—and the irritation of the audience's nervous system (the theater of cruelty); "supernatural images" in the consciousness of the audience—hallucinations and terror leading to types of phenomena such as: *katharsis*, ecstasy, and the psychotherapeutic effect—"the bubonic plague"; and finally the achievement of the goal of the ritual: the approach to the spiritual sphere, to metaphysical issues, the collective "return to abstraction."

In the eighth sphere there occurs a sort of magical reconciliation of the intellect (catharsis), psychology (ecstasy) and society (psychotherapy), so radically spurned at the starting point.

An essential remark: the graphic representation of the model of the "Magical Theater" is not, because it cannot be, a definitive rendering of Artaud's vision, regardless of belief in or doubt about the systematic nature of his thought. As Henri Gouhier wrote: "Cosmic life, always the essence of my essence through the establishment of my nature, which today is concealed, repressed, and rejected by culture . . . is inherent in Artaud's thought."[117]

Importantly, the linking of the material basis of the theatrical work or, more broadly, theatrical action, to intervention in the psyches of the participants, both actors and audience, determines the distinctness of Artaud within the model concept of the Balinese spectacle and its attractiveness to the theater artists of the 1960s and 1970s (Grotowski, for example).

Artaud seems to have expressed more fully and more dramatically than anyone else, as proven through his own suffering, the desire for a theater that engages actors and spectators and is subjugated to magic and ritual, a theater in which man encounters his great passions and anxieties, which hypnotizes him and sweeps him up in a sort of "vortex of higher forces."

It is worth emphasizing the anti-Cartesianism of Artaud, who had affinities with the tradition of modern irrationalism initiated by Bergson.[118] Coming out against the Renaissance as the source of rationalism and

---

[117] H. Gouhier, *Antonin Artaud et l'essence du théâtre*, Paris 1974, 22, 31.
[118] See J. Derrida, *L'écriture et la différence*, Paris 1967, 267.

The legacy of symbolism: Artaud's magical model

condemning the consequences of Cartesian dualism, Artaud was the visionary of the New Theater—who unequivocally and most radically refuted one of the foundations of modern European theater. Instead of dividing the intellect from the "bodily machine," as Descartes wanted, "We must insist upon the idea of culture-in-action, of culture growing within us like a new organ, a sort of second breath."[119]

With Artaud, the deliberate rejection of the psychological theater in which the word is an instrument resulted from the condemnation of western rationalism and the delusion of understanding man and the world that it produced. Artaud's anti-Cartesianism modified above all the concept of acting, in the postulates for the practical elimination of the contradiction between soul and body.

This was supposed to be accomplished through action in a trance state: "in agreement with the cosmic forces," based on a conviction about the necessity of "faith in the fluid materiality of the soul" (which ensured "control over the passions") and resulted in the end from the struggle against "the utilitarianism of the word (as a vehicle for concepts) and physical action."[120]

Hidden behind this were highly practical recipes and means for acting (indeed taken up fruitfully by the post-Artaud theater).[121] Above all—the creation of a new idiom of space and movement: "the search for gestures independent of the meaning of words, gesture/signs similar to those that occur in oriental theater." Second—the creation of a new theatrical entity based on "life full of passion and convulsions." Third—the propagating of work by the actors on their own bodies "from the inside," the deliberate application of breathing (it is "because the actor's breathing penetrates the body of the theatrical character, endowing it with life") and the "music of speech, which directly addresses the subconscious."

According to Odette Aslan,

"The journey that Artaud makes inside his own body has . . . a deliberately biological, genetic character: 'the body is in possession of breathing and . . . breathing is in possession of the body . . . Within the body is a level of pressure, comminution,

---

[119] A. Artaud, *The Theater and Its Double*, 8.
[120] J. Błoński, *Artaud i teatr magiczny*, 20, 22, 29.
[121] O. Aslan, *l'Acteur au XXe siècle*.

opaque density, the most intense repulsion, so as to leave far behind all philosophy, all dialectics."[122]

Artaud dreamed of making the word concrete and objectifying it—making it equal in its functions and rights with the other elements of the spectacle. What fascinated him in the Balinese theater was "a state prior to language and which can choose its own: music, gestures, movements, words."[123]

In the world of gestures, Artaud propounded "the return to primal—if not to say animalistic—reactions. Faces should be covered with masks or resemble masks . . . Gestures should have their own language, making up for the inadequacies of words."[124]

And at the same time he appealed to geometric patterns in describing scenographic compositions or the behavior and appearance of actors. "They are like huge insects full of lines and segments drawn to connect them with an unknown natural perspective of which they seem nothing more than, a kind of detached geometry"[125] (remaining in this respect under the spell of ideas deriving straight from the Renaissance).

Through the measure of his ambitions, Artaud seemed in a certain sense to diminish the significance of the efforts of other Reformers who were his contemporaries to break down the box stage and adapt theatrical conventions to the era of cinema and mass social movements. What concerned the author of *The Theater and Its Double* was the creation of the system of New Metaphysics, of which the Theater of Cruelty would be at once both the manifesto and revelation: "a theater in which violent physical images crush and hypnotize the sensibility of the spectator seized by the theater as by a whirlwind of higher forces . . . A theater that induces trance."[126]

> "Artaud," wrote Odette Aslan, "reminded us of the requirements of serious, metaphysical theater on the Eastern model, suggesting the violence and aggressiveness of expression, in search of organic breathing and the organic scream. He

---

[122] Ibid. The quote from Artaud comes from *Le Théâtre et la Science*, "L'Arbaléte" 13 (1948), 22.
[123] A. Artaud, *The Theater and Its Double*, 62.
[124] O. Aslan, *l'Acteur au XXe siècle*.
[125] A. Artaud, *On the Balinese Theater*, 64.
[126] A. Artaud, *The Theater and Its Double*, 83.

taught us, finally, to examine ourselves and—if it can be put this way—to devote ourselves to that examination."[127]

Artaud's successors would engage more or less systematically in studies of the contemplative and theatrical-religious techniques of the Far East.

After Craig and Artaud, the "return to the sources of the theater" does not, therefore, mean the refreshing or reconstruction of theatrical convention, but rather a scientific inquiry into the pre-cultural state, into the shared mythical origins of all cultures.

---

[127] O. Aslan, *l'Acteur au XXe siècle*.

THE LEGACY OF NATURALISM: BRECHT'S IDEOLOGICAL MODEL

"Rethéâtraliser le théâtre! Le théâtre pour le théâtre!" ("Retheatricalize the theater! Theater for the sake of theater!") rang the epigraph of Georg Fuchs's 1909 *Revolution in the Theater*.[128] It became the battle cry of the third phase of the search for the New Theater at the turn of the 19th and 20th centuries (the return to the arbitrary conventionality of theatrical art), which emerged after the experiences of naturalism and symbolism, and after Appia and Craig had placed the problem of the actor at the center of the aesthetics of the New Theater. Georg Fuchs, director of the Künstlertheater in Munich (1908–1914) and other proponents of the retheatricalization of the theater: such as Nikolai Evreinov (creator of the mass spectacle *The Storming of the Winter Palace* in 1920 for 100,000 spectators) and Jacques Copeau (founder in 1913 of the Parisian Théâtre du Vieux-Colombier), were linked with the earlier reformers by the categorical renunciation of all illusionism in the theater. They differed from the naturalists and the first symbolists in the absolutization of the conventionality of the scenic art, and from Craig and Appia by treating the plays not as aesthetic objects, but as chances for the creative interaction of stage and audience.

It is also possible, however, to discern in this phase a continuation of the antinomies of the entire movement, so visible in the original naturalist-symbolist synchronicity. On this occasion it is a matter of reconciling the post-symbolist principle of indirect presentation or re-presentation with reflections on the essence of the effect of the play on the audience as derived from the scientific postulates of naturalism,

---

[128] G. Fuchs, *Die Revolution des Theaters*, München and Leipzig 1909.

and on the "theatricality instinct" (based on transformational rules). According to Evreinov, this latter was assumed to be a natural and primal human instinct, and at the same time the source of all art[129] (as proved by the psychology of play, especially among children; the anthropology that described the ritual foundations of primitive culture; and finally the "theater of historical events," such as those of the Napoleonic era).

This is why the proponents of "re-theatricalization" regarded the idea of the "return to the sources," popular at the time, as a creative use of historical theatrical conventions—the Shakespearean theater, *commedia dell'arte*, and also Japanese theater, which Europe was then discovering. In accordance with the naturalist-symbolic postulate of "truth," however, the understanding of conventions as arbitrary, the collusion of actors and spectators as to the theatrical nature of the presented world, was not an end in itself. "Re-theatricalization" did not, after all, mean a disinterested play of conventions and forms within the domain of an ahistorically conceived tradition. The privileging of the arbitrary resulted from deeper reflections on the essence of the dramatic experience in the theater. This is why the concept of "truth" began from this point on to be associated not so much with the principle of theatrical illusion or the re-creation or evocation of a different "authentic" reality, but rather with the theatrical semiosis or sign process, of which the spectators are active co-creators.

In the third phase of the search for the New Theater, the postulate of "re-theatricalization" included a "fourth creator" within the newly defined work of theatrical art—the spectator, to whom an active role as co-interpreter was assigned. It was Vsevolod Meyerhold (derived from the Moscow Art Theater, in the years 1923–1938 he directed his own stage in Moscow called the Meyerhold Theater) who went the farthest in this direction at the time. Over time there was less and less reference to the delusions of the "autonomists," who dreamed of a work of theater art so distinct and divided from the context of reality that its existence did not even require an audience (as long as it had the essential, active co-presence of the theater artist/stage manager). The emergence of an interested audience with the desired reactions was influenced by the increasingly close connection between the theater and politics. On the

---

[129] N. Evreinov, *Teatr kak takovoi*, Berlin 1923, 38–57.

THE DREAMS OF "INHIBITED PRACTITIONERS"

Russian and German stages, "re-theatricalized" naturalism took on expressionistic forms.

> "Expressionism," according to Styan, "could identify any play or production that departed from realism and showed life in a highly personal, idiosyncratic manner, the form of the play 'expressing' its content ... Of all the dramatic modes of this [twentieth] century, none has proved more accommodating."[130]

This surely resulted in the revolutionary attractiveness of the theoretical concepts of Meyerhold and Brecht, which arose in Bolshevik Russia and rebellious Germany. Both theories panned out in practice, achieving notable successes. It was probably Meyerhold who was most consistent (at least theoretically) in treating the theatrical performance not as an autonomous work, but rather as a "message." He offers an unequivocal interpretation of this idea in his famous 1930 lecture "The Reconstruction of the Theater." He asserted that the "The author and the director provide no more than the framework ... the final realization and consolidation of the production is carried out by the audience in co-operation with the actor."[131]

Beyond this, Meyerhold postulated (and in this he drew closer to Brecht) that by way of its action the performance compelled the audience to make concrete suggestions. A mass audience was thus invited to participate, but with revolutionary ideas prepared in advance.

This was to be supported in theory and practice by Meyerhold's development of a new type of performance "of a revolutionary form" for conveying "revolutionary contents." Meyerhold deliberately and consistently destroyed the geometry of place, plot, and action of the traditional theater, proposing "the 'cinefication' of the theater" ("We shall stage productions which will attract just as many spectators as the cinema"[132]). The box stage must be liquidated once and for all, he proclaimed ("the proletariat is not interested in so-called 'intimate' or

---

[130] J. L. Styan, *Modern Drama in Theory and Practice*, Vol. 3: *Symbolism, Expressionism and Epic Theatre*, Cambridge 1986, 1, 2.

[131] V. Meyerhold, *The Reconstruction of the Theatre*, in: *Twentieth Century Theatre: A Sourcebook*, ed. R. Drain, London 1995, 185.

[132] Ibid., 184.

'chamber' theaters"[133]). This decision determined the basic assumptions of Meyerhold's "reconstruction":
1. in opposition to the ennui-inducing system of the unity of place—the real dynamics of performance on the new stage, expanded outside the portal and furnished with movable horizontal and vertical platforms;
2. in opposition to the unity of character—a method of transforming acting: actors will play a whole gamut of roles;
3. in opposition to the pseudo-classical unity of action and time—a new dramaturgy (including adaptations!) based on episodes.

These assumptions were accompanied by a peculiar transformation of Wagner's idea: the vision of the Theater of Synthesis, in which it was necessary to take advantage of all the means existing in other arts and use the organic alloy to have an effect on the audience. A significant shift is visible in this formulation—the ideal of the Theater of Synthesis is replaced by the theater of synthetic effect. The selection of the plays that constitute the ingredients of that "alloy" is completely non-Wagnerian: musical theater, cinematographer, revue. Similarly, the showpieces of the dramatic and opera actor, the dancer and the tightrope walker, the gymnast and the clown were to intermingle in the acting.

Meyerhold wanted acting to be based on a series of rhythmical repetitions of a given movement in space. After all, the fate of the theater, as he stressed, should depend on the actor—the main causative force, along with the playwright, in deciding on the transmission of the ideological burden. (Meyerhold the theorist minimizes the role of the director, emphasizing Meyerhold the stage manager and adapter). It was from the need to undertake such an acting task that the famous concept of "biomechanics" arose.

According to Meyerhold, the art of acting is the creation of a visual form in space, or more precisely the quasi-musical visual and verbal organization of a sketch of a role. The precisely developed and maintained form of the movement hints at the ineluctably necessary feeling and stimulates specific experiences. Movement based on the principles of

---

[133] Ibid.

"biomechanics," through the physical positions and situations defined in the partitura ("points of arousal") are the proper road to the soul, to psychology. The body should become "an ideal musical instrument" in the hands of the actors themselves.

In theatrical practice, the "biomechanics" method is a continual transition from what is "external," what is expressed by physical, rhythmically organized movement (easily grasped and therefore capable of fixation for unvarying repetition) toward the "internal," which, even if it can be made rational, is not always completely palpable (and in practical terms can never be fixed for unvarying repetition in any way). "Biomechanics" was supposed to provide a guarantee that the actor, making his body into an instrument that reacted the same way every time, would be equally obedient to the aesthetic (and ideological) ideas that the theater artist wished to bring into being. Meyerhold was thus one of those utopian reformers who wanted to remove randomness of forms, emotions, and meaning from the stage.

The theatrical ideas of Bertolt Brecht (the author of dramas that were already famous in the 1920s, an emigrant during the Nazi era and in 1949 the creator of the famous Berliner Ensemble theater in East Berlin) depended to a large degree on the heritage of naturalism and the development of expressionism (he accepted, for instance, the traditional box stage). Brecht the playwright profitably exploited the expressionist technique of the station drama, except that the station/stages of recognition were intended for the audience, and not the protagonist. The necessity of taking account of the point of view of the activated beholders resulted from ideological assumptions: "The spectator was no longer in any way allowed to submit to an experience uncritically (and without practical consequences)."[134]

In his presentation of the "image of the world," Brecht was a naturalist with a Marxist orientation (he placed his trust in the belief that so-called "objective" conditions determine thought and action). In the theater, however, he dismissed naturalistic allusion and wanted to replace emotional didacticism with intellectual didacticism. In the place of interpersonal

---

[134] B. Brecht, *Theatre for Pleasure or Theatre for Instruction*, in: *Twentieth Century Theatre: A Sourcebook*, ed. R. Drain, London 1995, 113.

relations on stage, he intended to introduce a specific bond with the audience, depending on providing them with prepared arguments for an "objective" recognition and understanding of the world around them.

This is where Brecht's rift with naturalism begins, and his ambition emerges of radically resolving, in Peter Szondi's description, "the contradiction between social thematic and dramatic form."[135]

Describing Brecht's renunciation of dramatic form for the sake of "non-Aristotelian," epic dramaturgy, Szondi connects the 1948 *Short Organum for the Theater* with Brecht's much earlier *Remarks on the Opera "Rise and Fall of the City of Mahagonny,"* published in 1931. The whole of Brecht's doctrine is sometimes called "the epic theater." The shifting of the center of gravity from the dramatic to the epic theater[136] was a postulate of relevance to Brecht the practitioner, the playwright and director of the 1930s.

According to the strategy proposed at the time, the strategy of epic action should be presented with distance, within the framework of the epically assembled episodes. The actor was supposed to pass adroitly from the level of acting to the level of commentary. All of this so that the beholders would reject emotional engagement once and for all, in favor of attaining objective truths the recognition of which would allow them to regain freedom—first individual (in the act of reflection) and then, as a result of the transformation of the world as received, social as well.[137]

Brecht devalued all plays—even those that fulfilled the ideals of the new dramaturgy—in favor of doctrine. He told directors to regard them as mere raw material. The basis of the theatrical performance at the time was "events in relation," intended to activate the "free" beholder. This was the purpose of the three most important "epic" procedures:

1. the type of external argumentation;
2. the degradation of the character, a particular objectivization of the person presented;
3. a type of non-linear, episodic action.

---

[135] P. Szondi, *Theory of Modern Drama*, 69.
[136] B. Brecht, *Anmerkungen zur Oper „Aufstieg und Fall der Stadt Mahagonny,"* in: idem, *Gesammelte Werke*, Vol. 1, London 1958, 153.
[137] See P. Szondi, *Theory of Modern Drama*, 69–70.

THE DREAMS OF "INHIBITED PRACTITIONERS"

The starting point—and the goal—was a predetermined "objective" ideological framework. Writing the *Short Organum for the Theater* at the end of the 1940s, Brecht already seemed to have less faith in the transformation of the received world, a certain recovery of freedom, or finally the guaranteed objectivism of the theatrical work itself. This time, he made a clear division into:
1. the raw material of the theater—the actor/role, the plot, but also the sister arts created by musicians, choreographers, and decorators (who impose on one another the stamp of alienation);
2. the theatrical means, or the "mechanical alienation" (the heritage of the epic theater);
3. the co-creativity of the arbiter—the beholder, who composes the action out of the impulses provided.

This is what Brecht intended at the time "to define an esthetic drawn from the particular kind of theatrical performance which has been worked out in practice over the past few decades."[138]

The post-war Brechtian model of the theater of the future no longer went by the name "epic." That word appears only once in the *Short Organum*, in the context of *The Life of Galileo*—from his own familiar revolutionary past, Brecht conjured up only this one play, written in exile in 1938. And it was confined in quotation marks, as an already historical way of acting, in which "the actor appears on stage in a double role, as Laughton and as Galileo."[139]

Demonstrably rejecting his previous epic orthodoxy, Brecht even paradoxically agrees with Aristotle in stressing that the plot is the soul of drama. After many historical twists and a wealth of artistic experiences, Brecht in his *Short Organon* made a choice similar to those that Appia or Artaud had made, and voluntarily played the role of the "inhibited practitioner." He chose the path of constructing a model utopia: "That is the sort of theater which we face in our operations, and so far it has been fully able to transmute our optimistic friends, whom we have called the children of the scientific era, into a cowed, credulous, hypnotized mass."[140]

---

[138] B. Brecht, *A Short Organum for the Theatre*, in: *Brecht on Theatre*, ed. and trans. J. Willett, London 1974, 179.
[139] Ibid., 194.
[140] Ibid., 188.

From the "old theater," he accepted then the Aristotelian principle of the domination of plot and the subordination of the experience of pleasure. Everything should "depend on" plot—the creation of the interpersonal and the yoking together of contraries, although the main purpose of the theater remained commenting on the plot and making it accessible by way of the appropriate alienation effects: "The exposition of the story and its communication by suitable means of alienation constitute the main business of the theater."[141] Maintaining the principle of pleasure in relation to the art of the theater was accompanied by the remark that the varieties of experiencing pleasure up to that time had become obsolete, and that it was therefore necessary to seek something new in this regard.

The new recipe added tempestuous social development to the dwindling force of the reform of the theater, especially in its naturalist variant ("The field of human relationships came within our view, not within our grasp"[142]) and the historical "alienation effect" (the A-effect or, in German, the Verfremdungseffekt or V-Effekt) that Brecht himself trialled in the interwar theater. The technique of the alienation effect is the only part of Brecht's old "epic theater" that would be of any use in the spectacle of the future.

It therefore continued to be obligatory for the actor to be sentenced to unnaturalness and discordant acting (based on the dialectics of the making-present and the "alienation" of interpretation):

> "In order to produce A-effects the actor has to discard whatever means he has learnt of getting the audience to identify itself with the characters which he plays ... so that the audience's may not at bottom be those of the character either. The audience must have complete freedom here."[143]

The idea also remained relevant that the beholder creates the action not out of harmonious visual and aural elements received in enchantment (as in the traditional consumption of the work of theatrical art), but rather by engrossing and assembling together the "elements of alienation" (or "free of the stigma of something well-known"):

---

[141] Ibid., 202.
[142] Ibid., 188.
[143] Ibid., 193–194.

"As we cannot invite the audience to fling itself into the story as if it were a river and let itself be carried vaguely hither and thither, the individual episodes have to be knotted together in such a way that the knots are easily noticed. The episodes must not succeed one another indistinguishably but must give us a chance to interpose our judgment."[144]

Here is a list of the new, theoretical requisites for the theater of the future:
1. instead of the illusion of an image of reality and instead of epic "argumentation"—the making visible of impermanence, "the unexpectedness of logically progressive or zigzag development" (according to the principles of materialistic dialectics);
2. instead of presenting the truth of character—dramatic or epic—the characterization of its "alienation" in a coherent image beyond the here and now; "The coherence of the character is in fact shown by the way in which its individual qualities contradict one another";
3. instead of the emotional involvement of the beholder and instead of the epic "forcing him to make a decision"—the actual reinforcement of the superior function of the beholder by granting them the privilege of composing the action from the impulses provided by the theater.[145]

Brecht at this point was, as can be seen in terms of his views about theatrical forms and techniques—as compared to Meyerhold 18 years earlier—almost a traditionalist. Instead of dreams about the dynamic variability of space, he contented himself with demonstrating the "mutability" of the world (in neutral space). Nor was he enthusiastic about the multiplicity of possible acting conventions and the perspective of the transformation of the actor. He limited himself to the gambit that he himself had tested of the "alienation of the character in the actor." Finally, he preferred to replace the temptation of *féerie* and the dynamics of varied episodes with the postulate of the intellectual reconstruction of the plot—in the mind of the beholder.

Brecht left behind another model of theater, taking account of participation by the audience, ready to be repeated unvaryingly. He believed that unity and invariability guarantee the subordination of

---

[144] Ibid., 201.
[145] Ibid., 196, 277.

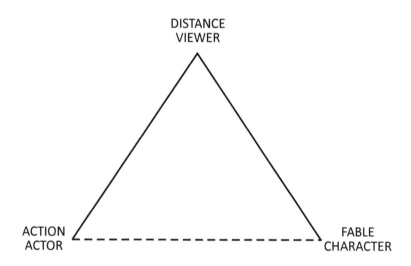

Figure 6. Brecht's Model of the Dramatic Work

THE DREAMS OF "INHIBITED PRACTITIONERS"

the spectacle to the rules of "objective" dialectical materialism. What he created in theory might be called a formal model of the semiotic activation of the audience.

> "For what Brechtian dramaturgy," writes Roland Barthes, "postulates is that today at least, the responsibility of a dramatic art is not so much to express reality as to signify it. Hence there must be a certain distance between signified and signifier: revolutionary art must admit a certain arbitrary nature of signs, it must acknowledge a certain 'formalism,' in the sense that it must treat form according to an appropriate method, which is the semiological method. All Brechtian art protests against the Zhdanovian confusion between ideology and semiology, which has led to such an esthetic impasse."[146]

The Brechtian spectacle, defined according to just such criteria, found a paradoxical continuation in the happenings of the fifties and sixties (where assumptions about the co-responsibility of the beholder and the transformation of the world were taken completely literally). Similarly Artaud is regarded as the precursor of the happening, because according to J. L. Styan:[147] "in Artaud's ideal theater there would be no written play, only improvisation upon a theme." This would make each performance "a kind of happening," as Martin Esslin translated Artaud's term *une sorte d'évènement*, and he wondered whether "this was the first use of the term which was to become familiar in the 1960s."[148]

And on the other hand, the trend known as "writing on stage," was one of the most important aesthetic and social manifestations of the Open Theater of the sixties and seventies. Styan believes that this type of "dramaturgy for assembly" has a future, stating that: "Lack of a usual structure made this form [of epic theater] the most adaptable of the century, and for this reason alone its offshoots will doubtless dominate the stage of the next."[149]

---

[146] R. Barthes, *The Tasks of Brechtian Criticism*, in: idem, *Critical Essays*, trans. R. Howard, Evanston 1972, 74–75.
[147] J. L. Styan, *Modern Drama…*, Vol. 2, 108–109.
[148] Ibid.
[149] J. L. Styan, *Modern Drama…*, Vol. 3, 194.

TWO THEATERS

Two opposing concepts of the theatrical work turned out to be the most durable achievements of the search for the New Theater from the 1890s to 1939. One of them treated the performance as a message, and the art of the theater as a platform that brings about a dynamic feedback loop in the relation between stage and audience. The second called for seeing the spectacle as an autonomous aesthetic subject, an equally entitled product of other forms of art, arising from the synthesis (or harmony) of ingredients that are named and conceived of in a variety of ways.

The proponents of the first concept (Stanisławski, Copeau, Meyerhold, and Brecht) generally placed literature and the art of acting at the center of attention. Improving and transforming acting techniques, while attempting to reconcile the truth of the actor with the truth of the role—and the audience (which played the role of arbiter, acquiring increasingly greater significance over time)—they accented the conventionality of theatrical art as a "language of signs," which either reflected the real world, or expressed a non-mimetic game with conventions.

Those who inclined toward the second concept (Craig, Appia, Schlemmer, and Artaud)—accorded pride of place in the theater of the future to a single artist, the stage manager, poet/musician, and priest. And they more or less openly sought exemplars of ideal structure in music, dreaming of something along the lines of visual musicality that would triumph over the temporal impermanence of theater.

New Theater utopia arose out of a conviction about the ineluctable destruction of the traditional box, but it was incapable—apart from utopian constructions recorded in manifestos—of erecting a homogeneous spectacle, universally accepted and corresponding to contemporary aesthetics, on the ruins left behind. The competing models cause difficulties

THE DREAMS OF "INHIBITED PRACTITIONERS"

in defining both the essence and the form of the spectacle in our time, and the very limits of theatricality, or the specifics and hierarchy of theatrical materials. Thus it is that the fundamental impulses (essential, aesthetic, and autonomous) that marked the beginnings of this process turned, after a century of trial and error, into their own contraries. Today, the essence of the theater seems more impenetrable, the aesthetics more impermanent, and the autonomy more doubtful than ever before.

THE PARATHEATRICAL AMBITIONS OF THEORY: FAITH IN THE SPATIALIZATION OF WORDS

THE THEATER OF THE STRUCTURALISTS AND SEMIOTICIANS: THE TEMPTATION OF SIGN PROCESSES

From a temporal perspective the rather paradoxical intersection of the thinking about the New Theater from 1890–1939 and the birth of structuralism is striking. The definition of the ingredients of the theatrical work and the specification of their mutual interdependence in the lyrical treatises of such visionaries as Appia or Wyspiański, as well as Schlemmer or Artaud, corresponds to one of the basic theses of structuralism, that "The true nature of things may be said to lie not in things themselves, but in the relationships which we construct, and then perceive, *between* them."[150]

Another thesis of structuralism, regarding the audience as the "fourth creator" (Meyerhold) or the main arbiter (Brecht), corresponds to the analysis of the stage—audience relationship: "A wholly objective perception of individual entities is therefore not possible: any observer is bound to *create* something of what he observes."[151]

This might be why, in the late 1970s, Richard Hornby identified the structuralists Stanislavsky, Brecht, and Artaud (along with the one living person on the list, the American anthropologist and director Richard Schechner) as most important for the contemporary theater.[152]

Yet in reality the most important theories of the theatrical work, from the 1930s, arose mostly outside the theater, and in all certainty the formulation of them was not exclusively the work of theatrical

---

[150] T. Hawkes, *Structuralism and Semiotics*, London 2003, 7.
[151] Ibid., 6–7.
[152] R. Hornby, *Script Into Performance: A Structuralist Approach*, New York 1987, 40–67.

practitioners (even the "inhibited" ones). These latter continued to reach for poetical manifestos or personal commentary, but they gave up on creating ideal models of the theatrical work in words, leaving this task to the critics and theoreticians of the theater. From the 1930s until the waning of the 1960s, things happened totally differently from what had transpired in the times of the flourishing of the box stage, or its reform in the late nineteenth and early twentieth centuries. A new profession came into being: theoretician of the theater—rather loosely, or secondarily, connected with the practice of theater.

The limited scope of the influence of the postulates of the avant-gardists attempting to yoke the theater into the circle of permanent revolution that was obligatory in the visual arts of the 20th century, the unsuitability of "-isms" to the everyday world of the theater, and finally the utopian nature of the New Theater model—all of this together determined that the new discipline coming into being at the time—theatrology or theater studies—began by compiling a description of theatrical reality according to methodological directives carried straight over from other humanistic disciplines, and above all linguistics, literary studies, philosophy, and to a lesser degree musicology and art history. It was precisely structural linguistics that held out the tempting chance of creating from the beginning a comparative theory of art and, next, a "linguistics-like" theory of culture in general.

As is known, the belief in the ineffability of language, which is always evident in the incomplete utilization of its systematic capacities, is one result of the differentiation of *langue* from *parole*, between the abstract linguistic system and the concrete utterance, discovered by Ferdinand de Saussure. It may well be that precisely this principle, adequate as it may be to the theatrical situation (concrete and ineffable at once), decided about the close connections between the twentieth-century theory of the theater and the development of contemporary linguistics. These connections become distinct in the obstinate search in the theater for the smallest particle of sense (signs) and the quasi-grammatical rules for their use (convention) and in the incessantly renewed need for defining the existential specifics of the theatrical work among other significatory systems.

One hypothesis that turned out to be particularly fruitful was that "the entire sphere of social behavior which constitutes the culture might in fact also represent an act of 'encoding' on the model of language. In fact, it might itself *be* a language."[153]

Jan Mukařovský wrote in 1940 that:

> "The possibility is beginning to emerge of a comparative theory of art based on semiotics, seeing that what is common to various arts is precisely the issue of the meaning-bearing structure and meaning in general, rather than the issue of the substantive substructure (matter, material) that, like sound in poetry, serves as a vehicle for that meaning."[154]

Behind these words lay concealed a clear postulate (of which the author was probably unaware) of rejecting the program of the autonomists from the time of the New Theater explorations. Structuralism ruled that the things common to different arts were more important than anything the separateness and self-sufficiency of the art of theater could show.

Linguistic inspirations further influenced the understanding of the relatedness and heterogeneity of the performance (and the associated co-creative role of the audience); the search for deep structures of theatrical playing based on the principle of phonemic modeling; and also the description of the very structure of the spectacle in categories of binary opposition (the most important binary opposition in theater is of course the differentiation of the presenting and the presented).

Janusz Sławiński was surely right to a considerable degree when he wrote that "the structuralist theory of art only took on a systematic nature to a fragmentary degree while for the most part remaining an open collection of views, issues, and hypotheses waiting to be developed, fleshed out, and verified."[155] But Keir Elam in turn, in his summary of the achievements of the twentieth-century semiotics of the theater and drama, stated that since the time of Aristotle little progress had been made in the area of knowledge about the theatrical spectacle—until 1931 when, in his opinion, decidedly new perspectives for scholarly analysis were revealed by two works published at the time in Czechoslovakia: *Estetika*

---

[153] T. Hawkes, *Structuralism and Semiotics*, 19.
[154] J. Mukařovský, *O jazyce básnickém*, "Slovo a slovenost" 3 (1940), 145.
[155] J. Sławiński, *Dzieło. Język. Tradycja*, Warszawa 1974, 255.

dramatického umění [Aesthetics of the Art of Drama] by Otakar Zich and *Pokus o strukturní rozbor hereckého zjevu* [An Attempted Structural Analysis of the Phenomenon of the Actor] by Jan Mukařovský.[156]

Even if this thesis seems a bit bold in reference to the accomplishments of the theater between the times of Aristotle and Mukařovský, it must undoubtedly be admitted that the year 1931 inaugurated a period of several decades of the semioticization of an important part of the theoretical thinking about the theater. It seems possible to distinguish three stages in the development of twentieth-century semiotic reflections on the phenomenon of theatricality:[157]

1. THE ANALYTICAL STAGE: the adaptation of the achievements of structural linguists, interest in the theatrical sign, the search for the minimal significant unit in the play and the attempt at constructing, as in language, a dictionary and grammar of theatrical behavior (which in fact deepened thinking about theatrical conventions);
2. THE SYNTHETIC STAGE: the application of the theory of texts in analogy to research on theater; attempts at formulating rules of audience segmentation and establishing "units of content" (especially according to the functions that characters play in the development of the action); creating "multi-levelled" systems of meaning, "fabular grammars," etc.;
3. THE PRAGMATIC STAGE: according a privileged position to the process of marking, taking into account the play as process and the co-creative role of the spectator, the analysis of the relation to code and context, taking up the methods of psycholinguistics and cognitive linguistics, as well as experimental research on the process of reception.

In the whole era of "semiotic imperialism," natural language was treated as the most perfect instrument of perception and as an ideal model for all codes of universally understood culture. It was expected to create an ideal system for dividing the world into units of content (thanks to

---

[156] K. Elam, *The Semiotics of Theatre and Drama*, London 1987, 5. See F. Deàk, *Structuralism in Theatre: The Prague School Contribution*, "The Drama Review" 4 (1976), 83–94.

[157] P. Pavis, *Sémiologie théâtrale*, in: idem, *Dictionnaire du Théâtre*, Paris 1980, 358–364.

morphemes) and a synthetic image of the world—in the syntagmatic series subordinated to the rules of semantics and syntax. It was also proof of the two-stage inevitability, primary and secondary, of the semiotization of all reality in every cultural text. "Every semiology of a non-linguistic system must appeal to the intermediation of language, and therefore must exist only within the domain of the semiology of language, and thanks to it," wrote Émile Benveniste. "Language is the interpreting element of all other linguistic and non-linguistic systems."[158] As Juri Lotman wrote, "It is natural language that gives the members of a social group their intuitive sense of structuredness that, with its transformation of the 'open' world of realia into a 'closed' world of names, forces people to treat as structures those phenomena whose structuredness, at best, is not apparent."[159]

As had been the case at the time of the construction of the Italian stage, it was believed that there was a chance of scientific perception and faithful reflection of the world in the description and creation of drama. Now, however, the perceptual medium was not algebra or geometry, but the model of designation built into the nature of language. Or, once again to follow Sławiński in calling upon Mukařovský's concept: "the relationship between the work and the world has become entangled with the problem of mimesis and treated as an issue in artistic communication that should be formulated in terms of 'messaging' and not of 'showing.'"[160]

In the semioticization of every field of art, it was a matter of solving the problem of whether the subject under consideration is, in the semiotic understanding, semantically coherent, and whether it can "model the world, using a language that is secondary in relation to natural language."[161] Semioticians of culture have, in every particular case, given an affirmative answer to that question, out of a belief in the universality of "secondary languages" and that progress in the analysis of meaning that is particular to the twentieth century as a result of the counterposition of the concept

---

[158] É. Benveniste, *Sémiologie de la langue*, "Semiotica" I, 1–2 (1969), 127–135.

[159] J. M. Lotman, B. A. Uspensky, G. Mihaychuk, *On the Semiotic Mechanism of Culture*, "New Literary History" 9 (2): *Soviet Semiotics and Criticism: An Anthology* (Winter, 1978), 211–232.

[160] J. Sławiński, *Dzieło. Język. Tradycja*, 238–239.

[161] S. Morawski, *Główne nurty estetyki XX wieku. Zarys syntetyczny*, Wrocław 1992, 71.

of symbol with the concept of sign. The sign was held to be based on reduction, to be a discrete element of a system that guaranteed semantic precision and functional "transparency." The symbol in the traditional conception, on the other hand, was characterized by an excess of meaning, density, and ambiguity (almost as in the nineteenth-century theory of symbolism, which glorified indirect expression).

Things were complicated, however, by the fact that we are dealing not with the direct symbolization or "marking" of the world but—in accordance with the principles of theatrical convention—with signs of signs and symbols of symbols.[162] It is worth noting that when one of the creators of semiology, Charles Sanders Peirce, came up against the perspective of a geometrical expansion of the number of categories of signs, he decided "not to develop his systematic division of signs any further," but rather "to leave this problem to other researchers."[163] In the theater, moreover, all possibilities of classification are undercut by the issue of the fluidity and excess of theatrical meanings—which obviously imposes the problem of the immobilization of meanings, the choice of senses, and therefore of interpretation. Above and beyond the universal rules of natural language, there appears here the problem of the individually differentiated "competence of reception." Another problem is the evanescence and randomness of the process of the semioticization of the theater, beyond theoretical formulations of rules of semiocity.

In this context, the history of the "theaterme" (theatrical morpheme)—the "smallest particle of meaning in the network of impulses and interpersonal relations that are formed in the process of presentation," as proposed in 1969 by Zbigniew Osiński, seems particularly instructive.[164] Osiński himself foresaw difficulties in constructing a model of the spectacle on the basis of "theatermes": "describing all the 'theatermes' of the message would be equivalent to the production of an infinite list of verbal paraphrases of particular moments of the performance. In

---

[162] See P. Bogatyriew, *Les signes au théâtre*, "Poétique" 8 (1971).
[163] See T. A. Sebeok, *Iconicity*, "MLN" 91 (6): *Comparative Literature* (December 1976), 1427–1456.
[164] Z. Osiński, *Interakcja sceny i widowni w teatrze współczesnym*, in: *Wprowadzenie do nauki o teatrze*, Vol. 3, ed. J. Degler, Wrocław 1978, 68.

practice this does not seem useful or necessary; in addition, it would be monotonous and unconvincing."[165]

One of the most eminent semioticians of the stage, Patrice Pavis, came right out and asked the question of whether we have to do in the theater "with the semiology of the staging, or the staging of the semiology?" He went on to ask "whether by chance it is not the beholder who really puts the text on stage, and whether he does not establish for himself the quality of the relations between the text and the representation," and "Whether the director ... is not by chance a semiologist creating his own personal spectacle, different from what emerges in the process of reception?"[166]

This semiotic anxiety results from the fact that theater is *par excellence* an art of excess—more happens in any given performance than any spectator can perceive—and more than any of its creators (playwright, director or actor) can anticipate and define. Hence the enigmatic nature of a performance in which there are so many loose, unconnected elements independent of any one messager. As Juri Lotman said, theater is a series of "conflicts over the nature of the performance with results that cannot be fully foreseen." And he added, "the theatrical text arises as a result of the collision of an exceptionally large number of factors with an individual creativity that destabilizes the structure of the text, appears on many levels and with the participation of many people who are not guided by identical goals and principles."[167] Roland Barthes used the formula "density of signs"[168] to characterize the essence of the theatrical.

In the view of Keir Elam, the work of Tadeusz Kowzan, regarded as fundamental in the field of the typology of theatrical signs, in fact adopted the earlier theories of the Prague structuralists.[169] Elam accurately notes that at the source of many semiotic concepts of the theater there lies a triple

---

[165] Ibid.
[166] P. Pavis, *O semiologii inscenizacji*, trans. S. Świontek, in: *W kręgu zagadnień awangardy*, "Acta Universitatis Lodziensis. Folia Scientiarium Artium et Librorum" 3, ed. G. Gazda, R. W. Kluszczyński, Łódź 1982, 181–182.
[167] J. M. Lotman, *Semiotyka sceny*, 98.
[168] R. Barthes, *Littérature et signification*, "Tel Quel" (1963).
[169] K. Elam, *The Semiotics of Theatre...*, 20, see also 19–31; T. Kowzan, *The Sign in the Theater*, "Diogenes" 16 (61) (1968).

typology of signs, derived from the findings of Pierce, such as the unity of similarities—icons; factual unity, a kind of temporal contact—indexes; and finally learned, institutional unity—symbols; as well as Jakobsonian definitions of metaphor, metonymy, and synechdoche. Juri Lotman, in turn, distinguished three types of sign in theater: verbal text, the actors' playing, and the musical-graphic text (and the lighting).[170] This was an expression of thinking about the spectacle in categories more of communication than of functional signs, in accordance with the more general tendency in the semiotics of theater.[171]

All attempts to date to classify theatrical signs in opposition to the postulate of functional transparency are in fact an effort to resurrect age-old, realistic descriptiveness. They attempt in a single blow to reconcile what—in the theoretical aspect—cannot be unified: classification according to physical materiality (such as stage lighting or actors in costumes and masks) with classification according to the senses of the audience (visual impressions which of course are dominant, and auditory impressions). They endeavor beyond this to efface the boundary between proxemics, kinesics and semantics through the involuntary immobilization of the sequence of the phrases of the spectacle. They place a functional sign of equivalence between stable and momentary signs, as the semiotician-philosopher Franco Ruffini wrote,[172] while also homogenizing the important and dominant with the secondary and non-essential (without doing harm to the global sense).

It suffices to summon up the simplest of examples: the attributes of monarchy—cape, scepter, and crown (belonging, according to Kowzan, to the three different systems of costumes, props, and hairdressing together with head covering) mean one thing in the tragedy of an ancient tyrant and something else entirely in a pantomime farce of the "peasant king" type. They are not the same thing when the character of the king is an autonomous protagonist or an ingredient in the subjective projection of the main hero, or a marionette-like illustration of a general thesis

---

[170] See J. M. Lotman, *Semiotyka sceny*, 97.
[171] See K. Elam, *The Semiotics of Theatre*..., 31.
[172] F. Ruffini, *Semiotica del teatro, I–III*, "Biblioteca Teatrale" 9 (1974); 10/11 (1975); 14 (1976).

referring, as in Brecht, to tyranny in general, the feudal system, or the machinery of history.

The classification of theatrical signs and the attempt at their practical application in the analysis of the spectacle cannot prevail over the obvious theatrical phenomenon of an excess of equally entitled significatory signals (the structuralist "redundancy"). Furthermore, it limits the effect of the context (in the language of semiotics: "the stabilization of the significances carried by the performance") to the role of persistent signals, resulting for example from conventions accepted a priori, rules of the game, or compositional basics that determine the direction of the interpretation of the whole performance (genre solutions and the associated dramatic motivation of the action).

Despite the appearance of objectivism, the existing classification of theatrical signs offers no protection against the sin of individual intuitionism in their application (which in essence has nothing in common with the extra-individual arbitrariness regarded as a model for linguistic systems!). Grzegorz Sinko was undoubtedly correct in writing that "given the lack of advances in the semiotic research in the field of significatory systems other than natural languages in the theater, it is possible to penetrate to meaning only in an intuitive manner, although many researchers conceal this fact through the elaboration and complication of a formal apparatus."[173] Yet even he ended up accepting the intuitive, semantic segmentation of the performance as the inevitable starting point for all theatrological description (positing only the requirement for the appropriate competency on the part of the one doing the describing).

The arbitrariness of the principle of semantic segmentation was not alleviated by the repeated attempts to create a "significatory macrostructure." This included the invention of the extraordinary and unprecedented concept of "simultaneous incision" [*oboksiebność przez wcięcie*—side by side indentation; next to each other through the notch] by Stefania Skwarczyńska[174]—in other words the formalization of the principle that theatrical signs formed out of stable material transgress the boundaries

---

[173] G. Sinko, *Opis przedstawienia teatralnego. Problem semiotyczny*, Wrocław 1982, 69–70.

[174] S. Skwarczyńska, *Znaki teatralne i fraza w komunikacie teatralnym o fabule dramatycznej*, in: eadem, *W orbicie literatury, teatru, kultury naukowej*, Warszawa 1985, 164.

of significatory wholes or entities (demarcated by signs made of fluid material, and thus shorter-lived and unstable)—and partake of a virtual wholeness or entity (which in a graphic model creates the effect of the "simultaneous incision").

Skwarczyńska—like Ruffini or Eco—accented the question, insufficiently taken into account by analytical semiotization, of the historical, cultural, or social context in determining the full text of the performance. She issued a reminder that theatrical signs are always "subject to decoding according to the rules of art and the numerous codes of extra-artistic culture."[175]

In fact, the role of extra-artistic codes that lend authenticity or, as some would have it, co-present, perceptualize, or refer to the macrocosmos, have increasing significance in contemporary theater. The attenuation of the illusionistic tendency, however, limits the possibilities for the application of analytical semiotics (focusing on autonomous theatrical signs) as well as synthetic semiotics to the degree that the concept of "theatrical text" fails to place sufficient emphasis on the pragmatic side without taking into account the cultural, co-creative role of the Peirce's interpretant.[176]

The developing semiotics of theater gave prominence over time to the pulsating process of creating signs in performance, where the most important thing is not the role itself but the process through which it is created, not the sign but the process of producing signs, not a prepared, "given" interpretation but its co-production in the process of reception. Only then did it become possible to treat theater as Claude Lévi-Strauss, the classical structuralist, had treated all of culture: as a set of communication games. The pattern was set by the Russian formalist Vladimir Propp, who created such a model in reference to Russian fairytales. His first analysis, which remains impressive to this day, led to the discovery of a finite number of fixed, repeatable structures, that is, the functioning of characters which not only recur but do so in a predetermined sequence ("the succession of functions is always identical").[177]

---

[175] Ibid., 158.

[176] See M. De Marinis, *Capire il teatro. Lineamenti di una nuova teatrologia*, Firenze 1988.

[177] See T. Hawkes, *Structuralism and Semiotics*, 52; V. Propp, *Morphology of the Folktale*, trans. L. Scott, ed. L. A. Wagner, Austin 1968.

Hopes were aroused for the penetration of the semantic depths of the theatrical message, without being limited to the recording of superficial signs. In such a conception, however, theater would be only one of many cultural forms of making present the "permanent structure of thought"—inscribed most perfectly in language.

In fact, the pragmatic approach meant favoring the semiotic analysis of drama as a linguistic work to which was ascribed the potential of "spatialization." Theater, fertile ground for semiotic categories, once again became a place for the "spatialization of literature"![178] In the most important works in the field of late theater semiotics—as opposed to the time of the Prague structuralists—an important role was played by literary categories touching upon the "logic of drama" or "dramatic discourse." Franco Ruffini created the concept of the "two-handed theater" as the sum of two one-handed theaters—the text and the stage; "the sound of two hands clapping is obviously not the sum of the sounds of each individual hand clapping, but the result of a particular kind of relationship in which the two hands collaborate as partners."[179]

There were increasingly widespread hopes that a perspective could be created for ending the historical "war of the texts"—written and theatrical (to use Elam's definition).[180]

The semiotic analyst Étienne Souriau had already introduced in 1950 a classical analysis of the dramatic situation with the use of game theory.[181] His functional description of the ideal structure of dramatic action has a counterpart in the model analysis of dramatic dialogue proposed by the British analytical philosopher John Austin.[182] Here too it is a matter of taking into account the pragmatic aspect of the utterance (utterances

---

[178] See T. Kowzan, *Teatr jako uprzestrzennienie literatury*, "Dialog" 8 (1991), 122.

[179] F. Ruffini, *The Culture of the Text and the Culture of the Stage*, in: E. Barba, N. Savarese, *A Dictionary of Theater Anthropology: The Secret Art of the Performer*, London and New York 1991, 238.

[180] See K. Elam, *The Semiotics of Theatre...*, 98–207; idem, *Text Appeal and the Analysis Paralysis: Towards a Processual Poetics of Dramatic Production*, in: *Altro Polo Performance: From Product to Process*, ed. T. Fitzpatrick, Sydney 1989, 1–26.

[181] É. Souriau, *Les Deux cent mille situations dramatiques*, Paris 1950; J. Błoński, *Teoria sytuacji dramatycznych Souriau*, "Dialog" 8 (1960), 81–86. See P. Pavis, *Dictionnaire du Théâtre*, 19–21.

[182] J. L. Austin, *How to Do Things With Words?*, Oxford 1962.

intended to influence and produce definite effects—illocutions and perlocutions) in accordance with the well-known thesis of Wittgenstein that the meaning of a word depends on its use in language.

Austin's proposal seems particularly useful in the analysis and identification of categories of drama in which there is no traditional action and the characters enter into apparent verbal contact with each other to no effect—with negligible illocutional force. This pragmatic treatment of the dramatic work staged as a structure built out of successively occurring situations makes it possible to identify aspects that have no content or importance, but rather depict a power relationship at a given moment—abstract and capable of being filled out with unending variants of concrete subject matter (Souriau) or made up of multilayered actions in the form of speech acts (Austin). In both cases, this is the "spatialization" of the literary structure, to use Tadeusz Kowzan's later formulation once again.

> "The time-space nature of the products of theatrical art," Kowzan states, "implies a specific functioning of the signs operated by art. On the one hand, theatrical signs are arranged in a syntagma, that is in a spatial configuration as a perceptible element *in praesentia* [those that are identified and classified by analytic semiotics—K. P.], and on the other they function in sequences that develop temporally (which is true of both visual and auditory signs) [this development is in turn identified with the fabular model—K. P.]."[183]

The category of the "spatialization of literature" would seem to be the crowning justification for the semiotic description of theatrical reality. After all, despite acknowledging the obvious differences between the sign systems of literature and theater, it posits the far-reaching adequacy of "spatialized" and "spatializing," thanks to the accepted primacy of the fabular element. Yet an analysis conducted in this way turns out to be a trap for signs of another kind: the transposition of the linear principle of dramatic discourse onto space-time (multidimensional) theatrical discourse.

It may be worth mentioning that Otakar Zich, who inaugurated the era of semiotics in theatrical research along with Jan Mukařovský, himself deliberately renounced the use of the concept of the sign!

---

[183] T. Kowzan, *Teatr jako uprzestrzennienie…*, 122.

Especially in view of the ambiguity of the psychophysical conditioning of significances coded or made present by the actor and deciphered or perhaps more accurately interpersonally felt by the collective audience. Zich was regarded as a semiotician[184] yet it was for this reason that in his analysis of acting, he wrote not about "designation," but rather about "presentation," thus demonstrating his proximity to Carnap's modern logic, which distinguishes the "language-object" and "metalanguage."[185] Furthermore, Zich consistently wrote about the dramatic art—and not about theater.

Zich's concept seems to be far more promising than the later "exterior semiotics" that segmented the actor's playing, diction, mask, and costume into different categories or varieties of signs (the synthesis of which defies description), and also less dependent on the pragmatics of drama, while being more focused on the specifics of what is theatrical. The structuralistic differentiation of the presenting and the presented allowed Zich to define the phenomenon of acting with precision: to discover the category of the stage figure (the famous *herecká postava*)—as opposed to the dramatic character (*dramaticka osoba*),[186] which also turned out to be both more profound and more interesting than the traditional opposition of actor—dramatic protagonist.

Otakar Zich advanced the assumption that in the theater, notwithstanding the endeavors of the poets of the stage who seek at all cost a unity of the phenomenon of acting (subordinated to literature or the will of the theater artist, synthesizing the truth of the character with internal truth, or harmoniously linking the partitura with the form of the spectacle), what we are dealing with is the fundamental duality of the actor (the subject of playing) and the character created by the actor (made present in the living perception by the audience). The semiotician of culture, Juri Lotman, following in the footsteps of Bogatyriev, liked to describe this duality with the help of the category of transubstantiation: "It is not only the actor who undergoes reincarnation: the whole world, when it

---

[184] See I. Osolsobě, *Zichova filozofie dramatického tvaru*, in: O. Zich, *Estetika dramatického umení*, Praha 1986, 382.
[185] Ibid., 382–383.
[186] O. Zich, *Estetika dramatického umení*…

becomes the theatrical world, reorganizes itself according to the laws of theatrical space, entering which, things become the signs of things."[187]

In Zich's opinion this duality of the phenomenon of acting should not be blurred; on the contrary, there is no way to understand the essence of acting without explicitly delimiting:

1. the presenting—or creating—subject, concentrating in the act of creation on physiological, "endotactile impulses," perceived exclusively by the actor from his internal perspective, the result of which is the "stage figure" of the actor, invisible to the spectator.
2. the presented—or the result of creation, the synthesis performed by each spectator from "auditory and visual impressions," from an external perspective on the subject of the acting—the actor—which results in the "dramatic character" (which should not be identified with the literary protagonist of the play).

Zich's concept, recalled years later, seems to herald the inevitability of the later failure of semiotics in the theater, especially in its analytical derivative and in reference to the art of the actor. At the same time, the continuing relevance of this concept attests to the significant and persistent role of structuralism in the development of the theatrical work. After all, structuralism (the ambitions of semiotics notwithstanding) made it possible to preserve everything that was exceptional and mysterious—not completely defined and approachable only through constructive investigative models—in the theatrical work.

> "The goal of all Structuralist activity," wrote Roland Barthes, "whether reflexive or poetic, is to reconstruct an 'object' in such a way as to manifest thereby the rules of functioning (the 'functions') of this object. Structure is therefore actually a *simulacrum* of the object, but a directed, *interested* simulacrum, since the imitated object makes something appear which remained invisible or, if one prefers, unintelligible in the natural object."[188]

The dramatic character, according to Zich, does not belong to the actor. It exists exclusively as a visual/aural impression belonging to the audience. The stage figure, on the other hand, cannot be seen by the audience

---

[187] J. M. Lotman, *Theater and Theatricality in the Order of Early Nineteenth Century Culture*, "Soviet Review" 16 (4) (1975), 155.

[188] R. Barthes, *The Structuralist Activity*, in: idem, *Critical Essays*, trans. R. Howard, Evanston 1972, 214–215.

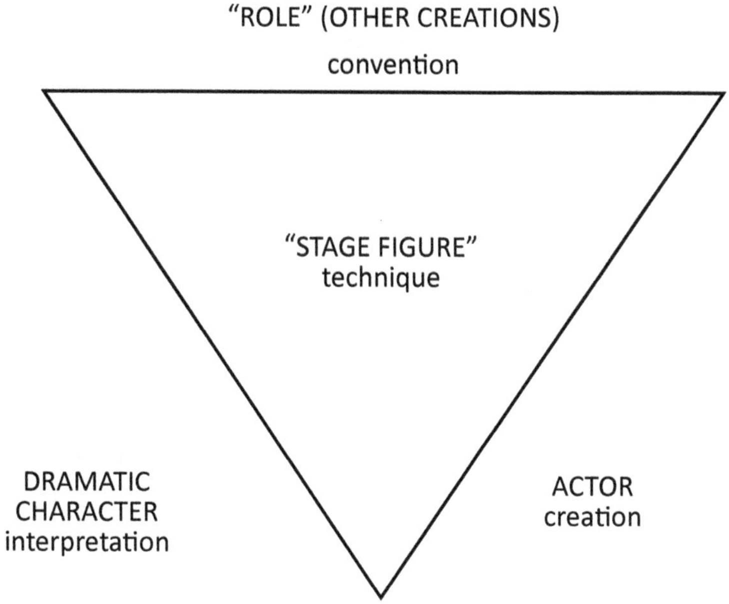

"ROLE" (OTHER CREATIONS)
convention

"STAGE FIGURE"
technique

DRAMATIC
CHARACTER
interpretation

ACTOR
creation

Figure 7. Zich's Model of "Stage Figure"

because they are the "internal-tactile impression of the actor," primarily bodily impressions as opposed to vision and hearing. In a word, the stage figure is, to the actors, the internal consciousness of the way in which they use the material and instruments of their art, or their own "living, thinking, and feeling body."

The abstract thought of the actor (centered around his feeling of the "internal-tactile impulses") is completely indifferent to the sum of the collective mental reflexes of the audience (centered around the dramatic person made present), not to speak of the object of reference, perceived completely differently in the "internal" perspective of the actor and the "external" perspective of the beholders. Always, as Zich writes, this is the obverse and reverse of the same coin.

Zich's introduction of the category of the "stage figure" made it possible to:

1. Define the essence of acting as a psychophysiological process at the intersection of the actor's "self" (the element of creation); the phenomenon of objectivization in interaction with the audience (the element of interpretation); and the "role," or the literary character, a potential persisting within cultural tradition (the element of technique and, further, of the convention of acting).
2. Unambiguously separate what the actor does (and their "self") from the entity they call into existence, which is perceived by the audience—which equals the triumph of relatedness.
3. Privilege the acted creation over the literary—in other words, to acknowledge the primacy of psychophysiology and the principle of physical incarnation over intellectual interpretation.

The limitation of Zich's concept results from the privileged role of mask, from the conviction he shared that the spectator perceives the result of creation and its synthesis in the form of the dramatic character, which derives thoughts and language from the dramaturg and physical properties (including physiological reactions and psychological reflexes) from the actor. In the real world, in twentieth-century theater and later, we have to do more and more frequently, from the point of view of the spectator, with the dialectic of mask and the living, acting subject. The spectator's receptive perspective has also long required a particular kind of dialogue with the elements of the synthetic "dramatic character"—the simultaneous analysis of what is mask and what is living presence.

Just as the division of consciousness into the observing and observed sides is important in view of the "proprioceptive perception" of the actor (Zich writes about this) so it can be borne in mind in view of the "visual-auditory perception" of the audience, and in some theatrical conventions must be borne in mind, that there is a divisibility of beholding into the distancing mask and the direct, living context of co-presence or co-experience. Both elements are generally present in the conscious beholding of the performance and there is no way of invalidating either of them (unless we are to be enmired for eternity in the imbroglio of signs).

THE THEATER OF THE PHENOMENOLOGISTS—STAGE AND SPECTACLE: THE CEREMONY OF PRESENTATION

A leading Polish philosopher of the 20th century, Roman Ingarden wrote about the duality of theatrical "presentation": connected with objects and situations appearing to the eyes on stage—and pertaining to objects and events occurring offstage.[189] Hidden behind this lies a suggestion of theatrical space: presented and capable of being seen—and co-presented, demanding supposition. The former was dominant in times when the stage box was a miraculous machine for conjuring up the illusion of "real" worlds, from the Baroque through naturalism. The latter took on increasing significance in the theater of the twentieth century, contending unceasingly like Sisyphus with the trap of the box by appealing to the convention of anti-naturalistic arbitrariness and the functional, non-representative construction of the place of playing, or the downright "naked stage" as defined by Copeau[190]—an idea next taken up by many other artists of the theater, among them Brook or Grotowski.

Étienne Souriau embraced anew this contemporary opposition of presented and co-presented space in the Renaissance slogan of the microcosm of the stage and the macrocosm of the world.[191] Souriau

---

[189] R. Ingarden, *Sztuka teatralna*, in: *Problemy teorii dramatu i teatru*, ed. J. Degler, Wrocław 1988, 276–277, see also: idem, *O funkcjach mowy w widowisku teatralnym*, in: ibid., 282–283; idem, *The Cognition of the Literary Work of Art*, Evanston 1979.

[190] See J. Copeau, *Texts on Theater*, ed. and trans. J. Rudlin and N. Paul, London 1990.

[191] É. Souriau, *Les grands problèmes de l'esthétique théâtrale*, Paris 1963.

noted that the presented and the co-presented in the theater are joined in the principle of metaphor; spatial relations shown on stage reveal an understanding of the truth about the world. The more arbitrary and undefined the stage space, the more expressly tempting the metaphor of the macrocosm.

The more defined and replete the space of the drama or theater, in turn, the farther it is from the Shakespearean model of the *theatrum mundi*, which posits—as in *Hamlet*—a hierarchy of earthly and non-earthly existences originating in the border regions of the Middle Ages and the Renaissance. "The age of Shakespeare 'moved toward chaos,' and the great mirror of his theater was broken into fragments," wrote Francis Fergusson. "And *Hamlet* can be regarded as a dramatization of the process which led, in the Renaissance, to the modern world and its fragmentary theaters."[192]

According to Jan Błoński, the theater long ago stopped presenting plausible events "of the world macrocosmos on the microcosmos of the stage, limiting itself only to the momentary *hic et nunc* of drama." This designates not only the shattering of the mirror and the fragmentation of theatrical worlds, but also the effacing of the "border between the conscious and the subconscious, the internal and the external, the plausible and the fantastic—and at the same time the symbolic." Nevertheless, thanks to the shared nature of the contents "that nature or more precisely culture have inserted into our minds," we continue to find in the theater a "particular variety of information about the world, about the macrocosmos, that extends beyond the theater" and that does "not 'stand out' in accordance with the laws of likelihood in the microcosmos."[193]

Błoński precisely elucidated the unsuitability in the contemporary theater of the term "mirror of the stage," summoned into being by the practice of the Italian "box"—based, as is known, on the principle of reflecting the external world. Thus, when Peter Handke described (and created) the space of perception (in which both the actors and the audience are to be found) in opposition to perceived space, which requires

---

[192] F. Fergusson, *The Idea of a Theater*, New York 1955, 153, 154.
[193] J. Błoński, *Peter Handke: przedmowa do teatru*, "Dialog" 6 (1969), 136.

supposition and subjectivization according to definite conventions,[194] he was appealing not so much to the Shakespearean theatrical metaphor as to the experience of twentieth-century drama, which introduced three new models of perceived space:

1. subjectivized space, infinitely open but at the same time finitely authentic, renouncing any kind of attempt at universalization (a model that has been popular since the time of Strindberg and the German expressionists);
2. closed space, encirclement, or alienation—as in the theater of the absurd or the works of the existentialists and in Polish theater most clearly in Mrożek—which depicts a character inserted into the frame of the action not as a result of their actions, but as a result of the influence of mechanisms that are usually mysterious and incomprehensible (this had nothing in common with the tragic contention with *Ananke* or a *fatum*, the realization of one's own fate—it indicated instead the sundering of the strict connection and interdependency of action and character that had been axiomatic from the times of Aristotle to those of Freytag and Szondi);
3. model, epic-didactic, quasi-naturalistic space modeled by overarching theories and a priori principles—for instance, ideological ones (most frequently, an "omniscient" narrator is the creator of this space, as in Brecht).

Contemporary philosophers have also been quite intrigued in the twentieth-century theater by the rules of making present on stage the para-theatrical, by the transformation of play into performance, and by the eternal co-presence in the theater of forms of existence and metaphysical values. An example is the existentialist Henri Gouhier who wrote that "presentation is presence in the present," and that the "double union with existence and time constitutes the essence of theater." The secular mysterium of the theater, thanks to the actor, "is a mystery of real presence before it becomes a mystery of metamorphosis."[195] Gouhier defined the relation of play and theater with the Claudelian term

---

[194] Ibid.
[195] H. Gouhier, *L'Essence du théâtre*.

"co-birth": "The performance is not so much the ultimate fulfillment as a new illumination of art: we thus continue our reading in another light, and that is the luminescence of the ramp lights."[196]

Gouhier expressed in existentialist terms Roman Ingarden's famous thesis that the stage play represents a 'borderline' case in relation to the literary work.[197] This idea prolonged by several decades the controversy over the theatricality of the play, encompassing the stagecraft and literary nature of the theater of the "spatialization" of the dramatic vision.

The main pillars of Ingarden's concept are, first, the analogical two-dimensionality of the literary work and the stage play (namely, the succession of phases that is analogical in both cases—the work of art is divided into strata). Furthermore, the stratum of meaning units, the stratum of represented objects is identical in the play and the performance, whereas the stratum of word sounds and higher phonetic formations, the stratum of manifold schematized aspects of represented objects is re-created in performance on the model of the corresponding strata of the literary work. Moreover, the side text drops into the stratum of word sounds; its significatory functions are taken over by the "ideal roles" while the stratum of manifold schematized aspects of represented objects makes the "roles" visible—real objects in the function of re-creation and representation.

The limitation of the problem of the play to what is after all a purely formal division into the main text and the side text, which constitutes the "double projection of the state of things presented in the play" ("the main text" always appears in quotation marks) was opposed by the proponents of the theatricality of the play as something differentiated from other literary genres through its being destined for the stage. Therefore both the creation and the analysis of the play must take into account the differentiated—non-linguistic—material of the theater, and also serve as a reminder of the necessity of placing the main text in a concrete theatrical situation. In the 1970s Anne Ubersfeld also enunciated the

---

[196] Ibid.
[197] R. Ingarden, *The Cognition of the Literary Work*... See J. S. Smith, *A Theory of Drama and Theatre: A Continuing Investigation of the Aesthetics of Roman Ingarden*, "Analecta Husserliana" 33 (1991).

view that the dramatic work includes within itself a "textual matrix of 'presentationability'" that enforces a specific kind of reading.[198]

Another analogy *à la* Ingarden is the similarly essential role of linguistic-word sound entities (which indicates the dominance in the theater of the dual stratum of language) in the literary and theatrical work, which only afterwards can serve as the foundation for the remaining strata of the work—including metaphysical qualities (the comic, the tragic, etc.). Another important analogy comprises, according to Ingarden, the identical sub-subordination to purely intentional entities (the "work of art is a purely intentional object")—judgments uttered in the performance are analogical to the so-called quasi-judgments ("sentences are only quasi-judgments") that occur in literature and are different from logical judgments.

Ingarden attempted to solve the problem of the appearance in the performance of live actors, who might be regarded as intentional objects, by differentiating:

a) the concrete actor as "psychophysical basic entity" not taken under consideration because of not being an ingredient in the performance;

b) the "role"—a real object (each actor, and not a concrete person) serving the function of re-creation and representation (this object belongs to the stratum of schematized appearances, made visible in the spectacle);

c) the characters of the play—a presented object, that is, belonging to a fourth stratum that is identical in the spectacle and the play.

In Ingarden's opinion, the difference between reading and staging a play depends only on the way in which the presented objects appear. Schematic and preliminary in the literary work, they are made visible through "role" and the associated visual appearances ("authentic" decoration, the localization of the action, and so on have a similar mediating function).

The "role" itself, however, remains a purely intentional object, while its material substratum is predominantly defined by the language of expression (only quotations within the dramatic structure) and not through the physical materiality of actors subordinated to the demands

---

[198] A. Ubersfeld, *Lire le théâtre*, Paris 1978, 20.

of a supraindividual "role." It is possible therefore to speak of the necessity of concealing the actor's self behind a unifying conception of mask.

Ingarden wrote:

> "The function of intentional designation, which is fulfilled in the read play by the side text [more obligatory than quotation, where the author-arbiter always stands above the characters—K. P.] is taken over in the theatrical production by certain *real objects* qualified in a defined way and manifesting themselves in suitable appearances, but not defined unambiguously as to their individuality ... These representing objects (actors) need not be precisely the real things and persons that find themselves *realiter* on stage on the occasion of a given *defined* exposure."[199]

Subordinating the actor to the role paradoxically associated Ingarden with the doctrine of naturalism in the theater. It was precisely the closed stage, which ignored the existence of the audience in the actors' playing (as opposed to the open stage) that he referred to as "modern" in his article *O funkcjach mowy w widowisku teatralnym* [On the functions of speech in the theatrical performance].[200]

Yet this is not the end of the list of paradoxes in Ingarden's theory of the theater. After all, in his theory of "borderline phenomena," he distances the theatrical work from other types of spectacle (especially non-artistic ones), in which he is obedient to the humanistic tradition connecting the theater with literature (for some reason there is no means of imagining a stratified theory of performance—for instance, the circus).

Another paradox results from the limitation of the phenomenon of concretization (n.b., a category identified by Ingarden) to the relationship between literature and theater, which overlooked what is peculiar to theatrical communication, namely phenomena of a multiphase nature and intersubjectivity (as was accurately pointed out in reference to Ingarden's thought by another theatrical phenomenologist, Dietrich Steinbeck[201]).

Yet another paradox, formulated many years later on the basis of American phenomenology, consists in Ingarden's misappropriation of the phenomenological nature of the theatrical experience itself, involved in the experience of the body and co-presence, which means the physical

---

[199] R. Ingarden, *Sztuka teatralna*, 276.
[200] R. Ingarden, *O funkcjach mowy...*, 285.
[201] D. Steinbeck, *Einleitung in die Theorie und Systematik der Theaterwissenschaft*, Berlin 1970.

sense of one's own presence in conjunction with other people (Bruce Wilshire).[202] Late phenomenology tries in exactly this way to present the phenomenon of theatricality in connection with today's convention of encounter—and the direct, mutual interaction of actors and spectators.

Ingarden's pupil, Józef Tischner, proceeded in a similar way but from a completely different position in his analysis of the human dramatic existence as open in terms of dialogue with the other person and intentionally open to the dramatic stage (understood not only as a place, but also as the co-presence of other people), and also open to passing time (interpersonal, connected with the question of God). Human beings—dramatic entities, Tischner writes—"domesticate" the stage, moving from the fundamental opposition (in the Cartesian sense) of subject (the active ego) and object (the stage) or, in the language of Husserl, constituting the intentional relationship of the subject of consciousness to the object of consciousness.[203]

It might be said that it is precisely the theatrical production that constitutes a perfect example of the collective application of the method of phenomenological reduction in defining the essential characteristics manifested in the phenomena of things and the examination—by way of contemplation—of the identity of things and the manner of their functioning in reality. In his study *Theater as Phenomenology* Bruce Wilshire comes right out and says:

> "The academic-philosophical use of the imagination typically involves only the mental acts of an individual phenomenologist, while theatre involves the imaginative use of things and bodies by a community of persons . . . We will regard theatre as a fictive variation on existence, conducted by a community of participants, in which each may surprise every other—as well as himself—with what emerges through their spontaneous interaction and involvement."[204]

Ingarden, however, regarded theater that was close to naturalistic conventions, breaking down the community of stage and audience and reducing the actor to a psychophysical vehicle for "role" and character, as "modern."

---

[202] See B. Wilshire, *Role Playing and Identity: The Limits of Theatre as Metaphor*, Bloomington 1982.

[203] J. Tischner, *Filozofia dramatu. Wprowadzenie*, Paris 1990, 14–15.

[204] B. Wilshire, *Role Playing and Identity...*, 15, 17.

Precisely in view of the diversity of attitudes in relation to the art of theater and the diversity of types of theater subjected to analysis, it is possible to speak of three alternative concepts of the phenomenology of the theatrical work:
1. the purely intentional "closed work" and its internal construction in relation to other arts and particularly literature—Ingarden's work referring to "contemporary" naturalistic theater;
2. focusing on the transcendental nature of the theatrical work as "event" and its intersubjectivity ("there are as many Hamlets as there are spectators") as a result of the intersection of "intended" and "assumed" events—Dietrich Steinbeck's work corresponding, for instance, to the assumptions of "epic" theater;
3. focusing on "contemplation through action and creation"—the principle of phenomenological reduction contained in the essence of theater, carried out in the imagination of a community of persons, based on the "involvement of man in the body and in relationships with other persons" (theater represents the correct phenomenology)—Bruce Wilshire's work, close to the ideas of alternative "community theater."

Strictly speaking, these are not three models of phenomenological reflection on the essence of the theatrical work in general, but rather phenomenological models of three different, mutually contradictory kinds of theater. In any case we have to do with theater of a different ontological status and a different means of ideal existence, subject to another mode of making present.

An example of the practical application of phenomenological theses (above all the determination that "no work of art should be identified with its material form"), without limiting the field of observation to one chosen theatrical convention, is Zbigniew Raszewski's unique theory of "theater in a world of spectacles" from 1991.[205] This consisted of epistolary reflections that are exceptional in the domain of contemporary academic discourse (but strongly anchored in the theatrical tradition), on the subject of the general theory of spectacle (the addressee of these 91 letters was a theatrologist and classical philologist living in the United States who

---

[205] Z. Raszewski, *Teatr w świecie...*

was perfectly familiar with European and Polish realities). The epistolary form permitted the author to lay out his theory at a "non-closed" stage.

He applied the method of phenomenological reduction to the historical observation of the transformations of forms of spectacle in culture, in order to isolate the "essence of theatricality" through a process of elimination and division. Raszewski's goal was not to erase the differences between theater and other kinds of spectacle, but rather to trace in the history of culture the genetic connections and dependencies that turned theater into a spectacle that was exceptional in every respect.

The methodologically fundamental problem of purposefulness recurs repeatedly in *Teatr w świecie widowisk* [Theater in a World of Spectacles]. This differentiation of purpose is, in the author's opinion, a condition for qualitative differentiation. There can be no art without intention—"by the very nature of things," art is a struggle against the accidental.[206] Raszewski's contribution to the theory of theater (inspired by phenomenology) consists of the formulation of an original, teleological model that defines strong, permanent boundaries for the work of theater art, which in its essence is impermanent and evanescent.

The starting point for Raszewski's theory is the definition of the apparently mysterious "S System," which is said to be a "certain type of presence created by a situation in which some sort of collective finds itself, not always voluntarily and always temporarily."[207] The symbol of the letter S derives from the Latin dictum *Spectamus aliquem quia spectandus est eoque nos spectatores fecit* (We watch what there is to watch and that makes us spectators).

The definition of the purposeful system makes it possible to define the condition of the spectator—in close connection with the "type of necessary experiences: curiosity, interest, fascination." ("Pondering the 'S System,'" writes Raszewski, "we are immersed in the sphere of unease").[208] The concept of the "system" itself is gradually narrowed: focusing (with a center of interest); axial (polarizing the participants); dynamic (thanks to the event being "of an uncommon nature").[209]

---

[206] Ibid., 204, 217.
[207] Ibid., 12, 15.
[208] Ibid., 18–19.
[209] Ibid., 13.

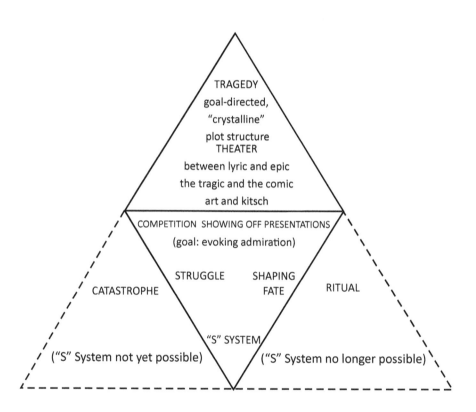

Figure 8. Raszewski's model of the world of spectacles

Further questions about purposefulness led to the designation of the following scale of phenomena:
1. catastrophe (fate itself—or "the dominance of chance");
2. struggle (or "challenging fate");
3. "the domain of activities for preserving equilibrium in community life" (or "the shaping of fate");
4. ritual (or "conjuring fate").

Not all manifestations of community life are equally favorable to the rise of the "S System." At the left edge of the scale above, it turns out that "S System is not yet possible," while on the right it is "no longer possible." Furthermore, Raszewski identifies two variants of the system:
   a) open actions (the people commanding our attention address themselves to the spectators) or
   b) closed actions (the people commanding our attention turn inward, away from the spectators).
Familiarity with theatrical conventions dictates an additional intermediary variant:
   c) "apparently closed actions" (the people commanding our attention turn to each other—as if we were not there, but with us in mind and for us).

In this final case it remains unresolved whether we are dealing with "a particular form of each of the variants" or only with variant (b) (both ideas appear in the text).[210]

If the preliminary definition of the "S System" made it possible to link the nature of theater to the nature of assemblage then the division into four domains of community life distinguished theater from accidental, purposeless catastrophe—and ritual, whose purpose excludes spectators (which is why attempts being made at present to reintegrate theater with ritual strike Raszewski as misguided).[211]

In the domains of challenging or shaping fate, Raszewski in turn distinguishes three groups of phenomena (competition, showing off, and presenting). This division allows him to flesh out the apparent initial paradoxes of the relationship between theater and deliberate competition

---

[210] Ibid., 22. See 25 i 49.
[211] Ibid., 22, 256.

(individual or group), and next to identify the goal of "evoking admiration" as "one of the few characteristics present throughout history in all varieties of spectacle." As a result of his teleological stance, Raszewski also—fashions aside—excludes happenings from System S.[212]

Raszewski begins his consideration of theater not from literature or text, but from a dualistic phenomenon: character, or that "human entity that arises from the image and likeness of man,"[213] and role, or the theatrical means of incarnating the character and making it visible. He defines role as a "complex of actions carried out by the actor in cooperation with a partner or partners according to a previously agreed scenario in order to give the theatrical character human form in the eyes of the audience."[214] The character itself, in turn, emerges as a kind of shadow—and a blurred, multiphase one at that—completely unrelated to literature! In this view, therefore, theater could not be the "spatialization of literature."

> "The process of the coming into being and fate of the theatrical character," Raszewski wrote, "is far more . . . similar to the birth and life of a tree than the translation of a text from one language to another."[215]

The principled polemic against the so-called theory of the translation of the play into spectacle returns several times in the book (for instance in connection with the "ripening—transformation" principle) until it culminates in the statement that the "literature or theater" alternative is categorically false.[216] As a way out, Raszewski suggests renouncing the concepts of literary drama or the quasi-musical *partitura*, which he himself had once proposed,[217] and introducing purely theatrical terms: instruction and scenario (the written version of instructions), whose purpose is the possibility of perpetuating the guidelines for the spectacle.

Raszewski rejects the alternative of "either literature or theater" (because "it corresponds to nothing in reality" and "does not evince any greater

---

[212] Ibid., 26.
[213] Ibid., 61.
[214] Ibid., 62.
[215] Ibid., 61–62, 93–94.
[216] Ibid., 231, 260–261.
[217] See Z. Raszewski, *Partytura teatralna*, "Pamiętnik Teatralny" 3–4 (1958), 380–412.

usefulness in relation to history").[218] On the other hand, he stands by the suggestion that it is possible to imagine a theatrical *partitura*, outside of natural language. He even considers the idea of the "super-scenario," more capacious and schematic than heretofore, and irreplaceable in the scientific investigation of theater:

> "The very attempt to develop such a 'super-scenario' would conceivably be a blessing for the advancement of research, if for no other reason than the fact that it would force scholars to make a hierarchy of specific elements of greater and lesser importance without regard to the requirements of specific styles. Without such a hierarchy the development of a uniform system of signs, no matter how few and how simple, is inconceivable."[219]

(The glimmer of the positivist hope for the fixing and objectivizing of the theatrical work can be glimpsed here—alongside the phenomenological faith in the possibility of making schematic views visible).

Also of a phenomenological pedigree is the appeal, in the second half of the book, to the traditional division between the presented world—inaccessible and indestructible (characters and their setting)—and the fragile, impermanent presenting world, the "focus of System S in the theater" (actors and their roles, or more precisely "speeches" and "directives" from rehearsals, as well as props and scenery). Not belonging to the presenting world, however, are the author, director, stage designer, or composer[220] (an important corrective to the theory, ubiquitous until recently, of the multiple transmitters of the theatrical work).

Raszewski distances himself from the structuralist opposition of *signifiant* to *signifié* by way of his conviction about the separateness in form of existence and the impermeable boundary between the two worlds. "After all," he argues, "it is possible to interrupt an actor, but not Hamlet—any more than it is possible to converse with him!"[221]

The necessity of the existence of boundaries between the presenting and presented worlds, and between stage and audience ("it is impossible to enter the presenting world without becoming part of the play"[222]),

---

[218] Z. Raszewski, *Teatr w świecie...*, 260.
[219] Ibid., 149.
[220] Ibid., 101–104.
[221] Ibid., 102.
[222] Ibid., 109.

nonetheless recalls the pairs of theatrical opposites, formulated by the semioticians, such as existing vs. non-existing (excessively rooted, it would seem, in naturalistic conventions).

Another classification of the ingredients of the theater also appears in Raszewski's letters: conditions that do not belong to the presenting world (that is, time and place—the theater building and the stage) and resources serving the presentation (people and things), as well as "INSTRUCTIONS for the use of resources," or "ELEMENTS of presentation and DIRECTIVES referring to their employment."[223] This classification is connected with the phenomenology of the multiphase and graduated nature of the theater—resulting from life (conditions) and turned toward life. So much, at least, results from the theses about the incalculability of the effect of theater and the so-called new context: "the blending of certain fragments of reality into the world of fiction is a necessity in the theater"—but "without lasting connections with the truth of expression."[224]

This problem had been solved in a different way by the sociology of the theater. For example, Elisabeth Burns[225] wrote about the necessary coexistence of rhetorical conventions, purely theatrical and authenticating, or connected to the practice of life in society. In the opinion of Raszewski, the necessary, temporary [!] blending of fragments of reality into the world of fiction, is "possible thanks to the cracks and fissures in the fictitiousness of the presented world"[226] (which could possibly be a condition for theatrical concretization, where fictitiousness is supposed to be more radical than in the epic and lyric). Theater, however, remains the "Kingdom of Fabrication" with the actor as "the main sower of fiction in the theater."[227]

Raszewski attributes special value to the significance of speech as the foundation of character and the main current in the history of the theater. He issues a reminder that the goal of theatrical speech was arousing the interest of the audience through inquiring into cause and

---

[223] Ibid., 103, 131.
[224] Ibid., 121, 116, 118.
[225] E. Burns, *Theatricality*...
[226] Z. Raszewski, *Teatr w świecie*..., 119.
[227] Ibid., 104, 122.

effect, explanations, reconciliation with life—pain and suffering.[228] Therefore, despite twentieth-century fashion, he criticizes the Pope of the New Theater, Craig, for the fact that the pure theater that corresponded perfectly with his dreams was not completely mute—"voices could be heard that delusively resembled human speech, except that they were unencumbered by any sense" ("I can even imagine it," Raszewski writes, "but I'm not interested in it").[229]

To place theater in the European tradition, Raszewski uses three quite classical distinctions. To flesh this out, there is his opinion about the "woeful condition" of the theater at the end of the twentieth century (and the beginning of the next): "relatively rarely has it occurred," he wrote, that the theater "fell so low," or had been "so vulgar."[230] First, between epic (or "the expression of interest in the external world") and lyric (or "the expression of experiences"). Like film, theater stands closer to epic (analogical phenomena of fabularity)—and thus, however, there is consent to the "kinship through fable"[231] of the literary work and the work of theater art. In turn, Raszewski treats the contemporary "lyrical" productions, for instance those of Tadeusz Kantor, as a "deliberate regression to the situation before the discovery of tragedy." They are, in his opinion, an expression of an epoch that degraded theater because of the universal devaluation of the concept of the tragic and the "decline of interest in the construction that created Greek tragedy"[232] (he leaves the tension between epic tendencies and subjective form, so typical of the dramaturgy and theater of the twentieth century, out of his considerations).

His second distinction, between the tragic and the comic, was intended to bring theater to life. As opposed to the epic "stream" (or narration, as in a novel or television serial), the deliberate composition of tragedy is best reflected by a "crystal" (of two types) or, more precisely, a "bisphenoid,

---

[228] Ibid., 244–245.
[229] Ibid., 88.
[230] Ibid., 154.
[231] See J. Ziomek, *Powinowactwo przez fabułę*, in: idem, *Powinowactwa literatury*, Warszawa 1980, 7–101.
[232] Z. Raszewski, *Teatr w świecie…*, 178.

known in Polish as a rhombic tetrahedron"[233] (an unusual modification of the Freytagian pyramid).

Finally, the third distinction sees the work of art opposed to kitsch, which means "an apparent work," as is very often the case in a theatrical production that, like other spectacles, "has no enduring relationship with the world of values." On the contrary, the breaking of these connections was precisely the price of the emancipation of the theater.[234]

When Raszewski is considering the issue of kitsch in the theater, his indignation surfaces over the "reckless showing off by contemporary directors" who now recycle the reasonably correct, aesthetic postulates of the propagators of the New Theater from the turn of the nineteenth and twentieth centuries:[235]

> "They were supposed to banish all egoistical arbitrariness from the theater, and they ended up ordering us to swoon over their present cleverness and originality, while providing proofs of vanity next to which the vanity of a prima donna could pass as a demonstration of quiet humility."

All showing off, Raszewski reminds us, "acts destructively on the properties of the work"; as can be concluded from the preliminary classification, ostensibly closed acts supersede open ones.[236] In this controversy, Raszewski does not share the delight of the post-modernists over the inclusion in the essence of the theater of the characteristics of high and low art: he comes down decisively on the side of the masterpieces.

Similarly—and also in defiance of theoretical fashion—he is in favor of an uncompromising hierarchy in the world of spectacle. This hierarchy makes it possible to assess each historical epoch and supply, for instance, arguments about the paradoxical similarity in terms of the popularity of certain types of occupations between Roman times, when chariot races stirred the greatest emotions, and the turn of the twentieth and twenty-first centuries with football in the ascendancy.[237]

As a historian of theater, Raszewski unconditionally acknowledged the necessity of demarcating the boundaries of theater in the face of the

---

[233] Ibid., 160–163.
[234] Ibid., 199, 227–228.
[235] Ibid., 228.
[236] Ibid.
[237] Ibid., 193.

dependency of this art on the world of spectacle, or, more broadly, the phenomena of social life. In his concept, theater was determined by the intention, common to all spectacles, of arousing awe and admiration; the purely theatrical phenomenon of the character, multiphase, and graduated; the deliberate subordination to fiction (turned toward life); the necessary aspiration to connections to the world of values; and finally the crystalline construction of the action.

Following phenomenological aesthetics in rejecting a purely material as well as a purely ideal mode of existence for the theatrical work, Raszewski never loses sight of the artistic nature of theater and its exceptional goal: the ability to evoke specific experiences.

THE THEATER OF SOCIOLOGISTS AND ANTHROPOLOGISTS: THE DOGMA OF CONVENTION

The invention of the box stage highlighted with additional vividness the problem of illusion and reality or rather—as it might be reformulated in the language of that epoch—the problem of falsehood and truth in the art of the theater. Through the eighteenth century, it was thought that a theater presenting invented stories is a hotbed of lies—in contrast to such respectable public institutions as the Church, courts, parliament, or academia, which had the vocation of serving the Truth—whether divine or human. Theater is often accused of false imitations of behavior and feelings in acting, and also of an unbecoming manipulation of the experiences of the audience. Repeated attempts have been made throughout history to exclude theater from the domain of culture. This might also be the place to point out the various anti-theater ideologies, such as those formulated by the Church Fathers or those created by Jean-Jacques Rousseau.[238]

It is interesting that accusations made through the end of the nineteenth century no longer pertained to theatrical conventions in general, but to a concrete model, which is characterized by extraordinary endurance, and has lasted through the centuries as if in defiance of the logic of history, and certainly in defiance of the logic of succeeding aesthetic revolutions. This is, of course, the box stage. The first attempt to overthrow it was made by the propagators of the New Theater more than a hundred years

---

[238] See J. Duvignaud, *Les Ombres collectives*, Paris 1973, 359–369; J. Barish, *The Antitheatrical Prejudice*, Berkeley 1985.

ago, and their successors, and later the theatrologists and especially those concerned with the sociology of theater. After all, the ineluctable evolution of societies and the necessary impermanence of "aesthetic dictatorships" made it imperative for the representatives of that tendency to formulate such judgments as the following:

> "There is a ubiquitous confusion of the concept of theater in general with that of the box stage," stated Jean Duvignaud. "This stage became at the same time a petrified and sclerotic *institution* and an intellectual axiom within which, of necessity, dramatic creativity expressed itself . . . If we question the right of the box stage to play the role of an absolute aesthetic model and the only framework for all methods of presenting man, it is because it strikes us as improper that this type of stage is divorced from the social experiences in which it was formed, as well as from the vital forces that endeavor to perpetuate forms that are already obsolete."[239]

In essence, the whole thing can be reduced—first—to the problem of the convention of the encounter between people undertaking defined social roles (in this case, actors and audience). Here, the difference between theater and, for instance, the courtroom, does not strike us today as so fundamental, and the relationship between microcosm and macrocosm not so dependent on the very illusion of presentation.

Second—it is a matter of the conventions of depicting the drama, or the contentious sphere of the interpersonal dimension, on stage, of the rules of mimicking, imitating, or representing life in the theater. In this sense—as the less revolutionary sociologists of the theater argue—theatrical illusion does not necessarily mean that pretending, pretense, or a false onstage reality are the inevitable result of the process of modeling scenes from the macrocosm of social experience in the microcosm of the stage (then the box stage could stop being suspected of expressing the truth of only a single, outdated social formation).

Illusion, for example as conceived of by Elizabeth Burns, "is only a specifically theatrical term for a process inherent in all social interaction."[240] It seems equally justifiable to ponder the element of illusion in the theatrical situation as in every interpersonal encounter, from the private

---

[239] J. Duvignaud, *Spectacle et société*, Paris 1970. See Y. Bonnat, *Le décor de théâtre dans le monde depuis 1960*, Bruxelles 1973, 9 and passim.

[240] E. Burns, *Theatricality...*, 17.

to the most official. The complete definition of illusion thus understood must take into account:
1. the definition of the situation;
2. the acting Person;
3. the other Person, who assesses or interprets or interprets that action.[241]

From that point of view the image set in the model of the Italian stage is similarly illusory, as is the situation of the "encounter" of actors and audience in the "open theater" model of the 1960s. Theatricality can apply to all behavior, as interpreted by others in relation to the conventions of the stage.

Illusion, in Burns's judgment, is the process of confining attention to those involved in a specific situation. Additionally, however, the process is essentially that of providing a frame of action (according to several assumptions accepted in advance). A start to tightening up this line of thought might begin with non-theatrical examples, by distinguishing three levels of reality:
1. "the 'pretend' reality of games, sports, parties, ceremonies";
2. "the 'alternative' reality of occupational worlds and ritual";
3. "the 'overriding' reality concerned with the deliberate efforts to change or defend definitions of the situation, the 'rules of the games'"[242] (best example: the fairytale The Emperor's New Clothes).

Illusion and fiction occur just as often in life as in the theater. Social life is inevitably conventional, because convention results from regular behavior, followed by becoming accustomed to the given behavior and indeed the expectation that what is customary (and expected) will occur in a given situation. This is why the analogy between social life and theater was so easily accepted and disseminated, the conviction that, on the one hand, theater is a model of the world, and that the theatrical metaphor, as in Erving Goffman,[243] is the best way of grasping the essence of all interpersonal relations on the micro and macro scale.

---

[241] Ibid.
[242] Ibid.
[243] See E. Goffman, *The Presentation of Self in Everyday Life*, Garden City 1959.

In an analogy to the three dimensions of reality in life, as presented above, Burns distinguishes three types of theatrical reality, three types of theatrical illusion:[244]
1. "direct appeal to the audience" ("pretend reality");
2. "ostensible disregard of the audience" ("alternative reality");
3. "involvement with the audience" ("the overriding reality").

All the three foregoing models co-existed in various epochs; the discovery of the box ensured that for a long time the ideal seemed to be understanding the theater as a machine for making an alternative reality present. In the eighteenth century (in the works of Riccoboni the younger and Diderot), there was an attempt to define the truth of the stage, the truth of acting, as the truth of overwhelming the audience: a good actor was one who could adroitly manipulate the souls of those watching and listening to him, while leaving his own soul in the green room for the duration of the performance.

This process culminated in the naturalistic convention that degraded the actor for the sake of the character, separating the stage from the audience with an arbitrary "fourth wall" (although the concept of enclosing the Italian stage had already arisen in the eighteenth century) and, finally, subordinating the theatrical illusion to the principle of imitation by offering the audience an image as close to everyday experience as possible. Yet even in the most perfect alternative model of box-stage reality, the theater retained its dualistic nature and was unable to demolish the foundations of its own convention, consisting of the fact that without ceasing to be themselves (itself), someone (something)—for a limited period of time, in accordance with the definition of the situation—became someone (something) completely different.

Burns calls the rules for presenting the world, the means of exposition which the theater has at its disposal (those confined to the illusory world of the stage), "rhetorical conventions." She calls those other conventions which refer to the world of values and social models of communicating or understanding (in the relation of stage and audience) "authenticating conventions."[245]

---

[244] E. Burns, *Theatricality…*
[245] Ibid., 32.

This duality of theatrical illusion (where the theatrical rhetoric in presenting or making present each situation is inextricably interwoven with the imperative of social authenticity) is explained by Burns as resulting from the genetic connection between modern theater and religious ritual. In the medieval period, European theater underwent a second birth, as it were, repeating the experience of antiquity, realizing within the framework of medieval liturgy the process of the structural division into actors and spectators and then dividing the presentation from sacral rigor for the sake of the relative freedom of making-present in the conditions created by the magical box stage that was discovered in the next epoch.

The division into stage and audience and obedience to the illusion of representation—or the whole process of the repeated birth of European theater (in its modern variant) brought about two effects:[246]

1. the rise of a complex of specifically theatrical conventions, or rules for depicting the world in the separate space of the stage (rhetorical convention);
2. and opening the possibility for the development of drama as a separate art, depicting actors and characters through the integration and synthesizing of aspects of everyday life that existed in social experience (and thus making the art of theater authentic by anchoring it in the practice of social interaction, as sociology says).

In the theater and in life, as Burns says, "conventions remove the load of 'knowledge of intent' from the individual."[247] There is no need to penetrate the soul of the protagonist in order to interpret his behavior toward others as natural, in compliance with the accepted norms (norms that, of course, undergo constant social modification). Agreement on the shared definition of a situation (in either life or the theater) need not be either spontaneous, or voluntary, or the result of negotiation. Burns states that "Consensus is a requirement laid on people."[248] The conventions of certain popular rituals, such as funerals, involve the acceptance

---

[246] Ibid.
[247] Ibid., 29.
[248] Ibid., 30.

of "a fictive, prepared style" in relation to "non-fictional content," such as the truth of someone's death[249] (this is a matter of specific, expressive behavior by the participants, calculated to have an effect, and universally accepted without regard to the authentic, emotional connection with the deceased).

The theatrical tradition is not a codex of principles more or less subordinated to the rules of illusory imitation, but rather a collection of possible ways of presenting the repertoire of social action. "For drama is not a mirror of action. It is a composition."[250]

The problem of illusion is thus the problem of a social contract that applies to actors and audience, defining the principles according to which theater, becoming a paradigm of human experience, aspires at the same time to the status of a work of art.

All theatrical conventions therefore "derive from norms accepted by those involved"[251]—in life and on stage (and this applies to both the realistic model and the most make-believe model of performance). The theater of the Far East remained closer to ritual and based its system of significances on the rules and prescriptions without which there is no way to understand the rhetoric of those spectacles (after all, the effectiveness of ritual depends on its correctness). The semantic frustration of European theater (a permanent challenge for all semiotics) results from its dependence on the practices of social life, which theater has been trying for centuries to copy at the cost of its own rhetoric, because of its need for social authentication (which is much harder to grasp within a system of signs and the rules for their application).

Contemporary anthropologists of theater have been seeking those "pure" conventions in the acting techniques of the Far East, concentrating on the actor's "organic body-mind" as an acting instrument, and not a means for a definite message. This is exactly how Grotowski, Barba and other counterculture-era theatrical "revolutionaries" have operated as prophets of the new acting, seconded by scholarly proponents of the re-ritualization of theater (Turner, Schechner).

---

[249] Ibid., 31.
[250] Ibid., 33.
[251] Ibid., 28.

Richard Schechner, himself a theatrical practitioner, emphasized the difference between the theater of the West, in which the actor concentrates on the interpretation of the text, and the theaters of the East, in which the performer does not interpret but rather conveys the "performance text," which is based on a system of rhetorical conventions.[252]

In the view of Richard Schechner, theatrology should not be limited to the analysis of the finished performance, but also take account of an entire seven-part cycle: 1) training; 2) workshops; 3) rehearsals; 4) warm-up; 5) performance; 6) cool-down; and 7) aftermath.[253]

Eugenio Barba, founder of the International School of theater Anthropology (ISTA), defined his problem as "the study of pre-expressive scenic behaviour."[254] Not wanting to study the application to the theater and dance of the criteria of cultural anthropology (or the study of the phenomena of spectacle in various cultures), Barba postulated the analysis of acting technique in the super-cultural dimension (techniques, or the non-everyday use of the corporeal-spiritual whole)—in accordance with the thesis that "in an organized performance the performer's physical and vocal presence is modeled according to principles which are different from those of daily life."[255]

"Transcultural analysis," Barba wrote, "shows that it is possible to single out recurring principles from among these techniques,"[256] referring to weight, balance, the use of the spinal column, and the eyes.

These principles create "physical, pre-expressive tensions." Or "an extra-daily energy quality," which makes the body of the actor an authentic and living presence on stage before it conveys any kind of message.

Barba drew attention to three aspects of the actor's work:[257]
1. "the performer's personality, *her/his* sensitivity, artistic intelligence, social persona";

---

[252] R. Schechner, *The Performer: Training Interculturally*, "Canadian Theatre Review" 35 (1982), 3.
[253] R. Schechner, *Between Theater and Anthropology*, Philadelphia 1985.
[254] E. Barba, *Beyond the Floating Islands*, New York 1986; idem, *The Paper Canoe*, London 1995, 9.
[255] E Barba, *The Paper Canoe*, 9.
[256] Ibid.
[257] Ibid., 10.

2. "the particularities of the theatrical traditions and the historical-cultural context";
3. the "transcultural, recurring principles" common to actors in various epochs and cultures—the foundation of extra-daily techniques, or "the field of pre-expressivity."

The first and second aspects mark the passage "from pre-expressivity to performing." The third aspect is the search for the biological level of the theater ("the level of the scenic 'bios'"). One might add: of every theater, but this level is penetrated only by the "third theater" identified by Barba, which is polemical in relation to both the institutional and the avant-garde theater.

> "The Third Theater lives on the fringes, often outside or on the outskirts of the centers and capitals of Culture. It is a theater created by people who define themselves as actors, directors, theater workers, although they have seldom undergone a traditional theatrical education and therefore are not recognized as professionals."[258]

A full model of these new investigations of the "third theater" was proposed by Leszek Kolankiewicz:

> "A sort of paradigm would consist of several pairs of symmetrical oppositions: on the one hand a cultural utopia (Brook in the theatrical version, Grotowski in the ritual version)—and on the other a sociological utopia (Barba in the communitarian version, the Becks [from The Living Theater] in the anarchist version); on the one hand shifting the boundaries of theater (Brook in terms of the morphology of the spectacle itself, Barba if it's a matter of the social context of theater)—and on the other hand the transgression of the boundaries of theater (Grotowski for the sake of religion, the Becks for the sake of revolution)."[259]

The return to the roots according to Barba is the rediscovery of "extra-daily techniques" in the use of the body and non-observance of the usual forms of so-called everyday existence (where the principle of saving energy and minimizing effort to achieve the optimal result is in force). The goal of what he calls "extra-daily techniques" is information: giving (significant) form to the body. The numerous and complex

---

[258] E. Barba, *Beyond the Floating...*, 193. See I. Watson, *Toward a Third Theatre: Eugenio Barba and the Odin Teatret*, London 1993.

[259] L. Kolankiewicz, *Teatr zarażony etnologią*, "Polska Sztuka Ludowa. Konteksty" 3–4 (1991), 21.

principles that seem to limit and hinder actors from India, China and Japan are in reality the elaboration of precise methods of modeling and processing the actor's energy. As a result of the many years of work of the International School of Theater Anthropology, Barba was able to combine knowledge about the capabilities and limitations of "the scenic body" in the theatrical space with the analysis of the desired "spectator's response" to the dynamics of the spectacle.

The three principles formulated by Barba refer to this universal acting technique. "These principles can be combined in three lines of action."[260]
1. alternation of daily balance in the search for precarious or 'luxury' balance;
2. dynamic opposition;
3. use of incoherent coherence.

In the first case ("alternation of daily balance") it was a matter of creating a situation of a constant risk to balance, for instance the *tribhangi*—three arches—position in classical Indian dance: the asymmetric bending of the neck, arms, and hips in the form of the letter S, or the analogous "sideways wave movement" in *kabuki* theater in the *vagoto* style, known as "realistic" (Barba pointed out that one of the basic poses of the actor in *commedia dell'arte* shows similarities with the principle of *tribhangi*). Other examples: the sliding step in Japanese *nō* theater, walking on the outer edge of the foot in Indian *kathakali* theater, or the schema of classical European ballet (resting the weight of the body on one leg or the tips of the toes).

Examples of the presence of the second principle ("dynamic opposition"): in Peking opera, for instance, all actions are based on the principle of negation: action must begin in a direction opposite to that in which it will be directed (as often occurs in life with drawing back the arm before delivering a blow or bending the knee before hopping); in *nō* theater as opposed to life there is simultaneous tensing and bending in a single movement (in everyday technique these two kinds of muscles never act simultaneously).

---

[260] E. Barba, N. Savarese, *A Dictionary of Theatre Anthropology: The Secret Art of the Performer*, London and New York 1991, 55.

The third principle ("incoherent coherence") is expressed through the difficulty of overcoming one's own body in long, intense training (to accept and prove extra-daily techniques that are incoherent under the logic of life). Freedom can be attained or mastery ("new coherence") achieved in extra-daily technique to the degree that it strikes the spectator as spontaneous.

When the actor violates his own balance, he becomes unsteady and creates a whole series of oppositions between various parts of his body on the basis of the load/spine opposition. According to Barba it is precisely this that changes the mass of the body into energy, making the body come to life. This is the origin of the first, pre-intellectual level of the dramatism of the actor. It is thanks to this technique, according to Barba, that a struggle of opposites arises within the body of the actor. This gives the actor a new architecture of tension of the living body and a new rhythm of the nerves—both elements are fundamental to the actor's pre-expressiveness:

> "The performance dances not only on the level of energy but also on the semantic level. It is its *meaning* which dances, sometimes explicitly, other times covertly and secretly, open to the free associations of some spectators, while ambiguous and unrecognizable for others."[261]

In this way, Barba sought techniques beyond the previous convention—trying to transcend both the historical universalism of sociological approaches and ahistorical postmodern anthropology. The goal of his "practical anthropology" was to define the bases of individual expression which help liberate not ready semantic structures but the subconscious creativity of the actor, brought by the living process of performance into collision with the audience's reception.

The association of freedom with rigor, the subconscious with rational technique, and universal convention with the "extra-daily" are paradoxes formulated anew, at the end of the twentieth century, of the timeless basics of acting: the foundation of every living theater, which apply "always" and "everywhere."

The privileged "performant function" decontextualizes in a certain sense the significatory nature of theater. But it creates a new convention—energetic

---

[261] E. Barba, *Four Spectators*, "The Drama Review" 1 (1990), 97.

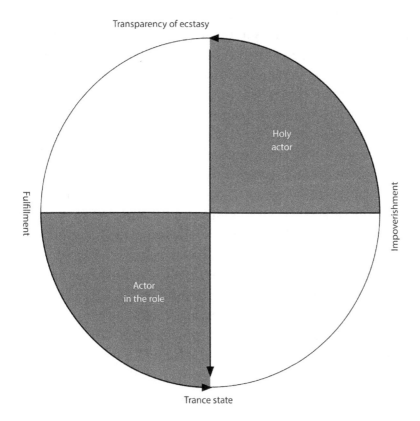

Figure 9. R. Schechner: Model of an Actor's Energy Engaged in Time*

* R. Schechner, *Performance Theory*, 179.

messaging, because the strong flow of energy rests in this concept on the corresponding structure of the performance, and above all the perfected technique of the actor.[262]

This Model of an Actor's Energy Engaged in Time, concealed in the perfection of acting, seems paradoxically to be more clear than the belief in the decisive power of significance as advocated by the semiologists. At the same time, it testifies to the undying power of convention, the foundation of all theater—whether the theater has grown out of tradition, or placed its faith in being a historical alternative to tradition.

Taking account of these paradoxes was the desideratum of a trend at the end of the twentieth century that deliberately renounced the definition of the autonomous art of the theater, refused to acknowledge Cartesian and structuralist antinomies, and rejected classification and schematization from the position of an absolute arbiter equipped with semiotic supercompetence or a sociologist submitting to the delusive charms of the objectivism of cognition in the humanities.

This trend or mental formulation, known as postmodernism, seems to be an essential commentary on the presentation of twentieth-century anthropological ideas in the description of the theater, already understood far more broadly: as *performance*, and thus not only as spectacle, but as every form of action. According to Richard Schechner, not only human but also animal, which situates all the problematics sufficiently far from not only the Cartesian tradition but also from European personalism.[263]

In the opinion of many Western theorists, the key to modernism (understood as the modern era or "modernity") was precisely the discovery of pluralism, and the associated, completely novel orientation in the world of man, sentenced to the rationalization of place and space demarcated by Descartes.

Among the most commonly compared consequences of modernism[264] are those in which the rules of the stage box can be recognized:

---

[262] See M. Carlson, *Theater as Event*, "Semiotica" 3–4 (1985), 304–314.
[263] See R. Schechner, *Performance Theory*.
[264] See V. Turner, *The Anthropology of Performance*, New York 1988, 72–73.

1. a particular spatialization of a world subjected to new human enslavement connected with technological expansion and the reconstruction of the landscape;
2. the introduction of a radical division into the observing subject and the alienated object (man as the "measure of all things");
3. the treatment of words as ordinary signs corresponding to the material objects of the real world;
4. the perception of time in spatial categories (the principle of linear succession);
5. the harmony of technological rationalism—and the protestant ethic; the elevation of the advocates for individualism and competition in a modernist society based on "rational" principles of authority and control;
6. the conception of history as a line of unceasing progress, as a history of the gradual self-perfection of man through experiments brought before the court of reason.

In the modernistic climate thus defined, traditional anthropology presented social reality as stable and unvarying, and more precisely as a harmonious configuration governed by principles that were logical and mutually adapted. This model, clearly, had little in common with social reality and far more in common with the ideology in the name of which it was formulated. American postmodernists regarded the whole Western philosophical tradition, from Plato and Aristotle through Descartes, Hegel, and Kant, up to contemporary structural anthropology, as an expression of the need for basing the image of the world on the determinism of a preexisting order (guided by ideas or a hypothetical structure). It criticized both poles of the Western tradition: radical individualism because it understood only a part of man, and radical collectivism because it understood man as a part. It tried to find a solution in the idea of *performans*, engaging and individual, and the social dimension of man in a multifarious process of many aspects.

The post-modernist shift in culture (and ideology) over the last decades has resulted from the need to reject all models that "falsify" reality (born, let us recall, from the spatial perception of the world). In return, we have been offered (in the works of Goffman, Schechner and

Turner,[265] for instance) the transformation of static space into a process, and have seen it given a temporal dimension (mutability, motion, etc.). This is different from the "spatialization" of time that Turner identifies as the essence of modernism. Postmodernist anthropology of the theater in this light was something completely different from all earlier concepts of theater (those, like all of classical structuralism, semiotics, or phenomenology, were yet to drown in late-stage modernism).

This can be expressed by Chomsky's notorious opposition: *competence/performance*.[266] Competence, or the masterfully ideal system of rules, which are used by the speaker—as opposed to performance, real language action and the inevitable associated divergence from the purity of the grammatical system of rules, resulting from the distraction of attention, gaps in memory, accidental enunciation, the intervention of the subconscious in Freudian slips.

The opposition of *competence/performance* replaced the de Saussurian opposition of *langue/parole*. On the one hand it introduced a "pure, systemic idea" (indicating Chomsky's hidden neoplatonism); on the other—the sin-burdened inevitable impurity—the performance of speech (in which the analogy with theater is distinctly present).

The modernist theories of theater, constructing spatial models, attempted to reduce the living, extra-sign—and impure—spectacle to purity and the unambivalence of the model of a machine to the production of meanings. Postmodernist anthropologists of the theater attempted to concentrate on what deviated from all rules, broke down divisions, destroyed pre-theatrical dispositions, all assumptions accepted a priori, and thence on everything that was the essence of performance, especially in the theater—sentenced to play a game with the accidental.

The postmodernist turn according to Turner consisted of the reversal of this purifying process of thinking, which from mistakes and accidents, hesitations and uncertainties, gradually moved in the direction of abstracted senses and rules, the division of plans of utterance (structure),

---

[265] See E. Goffman, *The Presentation of Self...*; idem, *Interaction Ritual*, Garden City 1967; V. Turner, *The Anthropology of Performance*; idem, *From Ritual to Theatre: The Human Seriousness of Play*, New York 1982; R. Schechner, *Performance Theory*.

[266] N. Chomsky, *Language and Mind*, New York 1968.

from the plan of expression (concrete realization), the activity of the creative subject, and all contextual dependency.[267]

The proposed movement from the abstraction of aesthetic models back toward the magma of life, in accordance with the concept of *Homo performance* (or: *self-performing animal*), gave birth to sometimes extreme relativism, the absolutization of subconsciousness—individual and collective—and the introduction of the non-human, biological basis of symbolism:

> "I am sure," wrote Turner, "that a biologist from outer space would find the various Terran life-forms to be made of similar stuff, a planetary kinship group, from biological amoeba to high-cultural products like the works of Homer, Dante and Shakespeare, Leonardo and Beethoven."[268]

The spaciousness of modernistic thinking depended on the monoperspective point of view, permanent and unchanging in regard to geometrically conceived models of reality. Thus, in the face of the box stage, modernistic theatrology invented the superarbiter: a structuralist, semiotician, phenomenologist placed in the audience with all his apparatus for catching and freezing meanings from the multimorphic multivariant performance. Postmodernism in turn looked to the multi-perspective awareness (the relativity principle) that corresponds to multivariant reality understood as a limitless assemblage of performativenesses: infinite, multidirectional processes with multiple variants.

Postmodernist anthropology posed the problem of the possibility of distinguishing significances—only through death, closure, and the freezing of process. Every bestowal of meaning on contemporary facts is from this point of view provisional and dependent on the moment of resolution, on the accepted system of values, on the structural or psychological perspective, and finally on the boundary marked out ad hoc by the subject. It is like the method of formulating the problem of competence in a different way—as a collection of existing rules, like the Platonic ideal, irrespective of its immediate, spontaneous, and unforeseeable realization.

---

[267] V. Turner, *The Anthropology of Performance*, 76–77.
[268] Ibid., 82.

The popularity in postmodernist anthropology of studies of ritual and the "ritual theater" (as the most discrete and conventionalized form of spectacle performativeness) designates after all the submission all over again to the temptation of the lost order and the order of dogmatic convention, identified with extra-cultural technique and by the same token easier to be re-engrafted to the theater of the West.

THE HOPE OF PERFECTION

Those among the twentieth-century theories of theater that grew out of the main currents of the humanistics of the time placed the literature-theater relationship at the center of attention (as if to spite the visions of the proponents of the New Theater and theater itself, stubbornly proclaiming its autonomy for throughout the twentieth century). The examination of this very relationship defined the real scope of the semiotics of theater (signs inscribed in the dramatic-literary structure were easier to distinguish and classify). And it also predetermined the achievements of theatrical sociology in research into conventions, understood as the synthesis of social experience in dramatic form. The proximity of points of view even led to the unification of the two orientations in a socio-semiotic formula.[269] Similar philosophical reflection on the theater (inspired by phenomenology or existential philosophy) deepened the understanding of the process of the making-present of literary phenomena (character, fable, side text) in the privileged, three-dimensional space of the stage.

The phenomenon of the transfiguration of the homogeneous verbal material into the complex multi-material spectacle was variously defined: as the "spatialization of literature" (Kowzan); spatial-temporal concretization for the sake of the psychophysical existential substructure (Ingarden); "the making-present" of drama in the here and now (Gouhier), the "authenticity" of social experience inscribed in the drama (Burns). But the non-spatial and extra-temporal linguistic materials were always opposed to the first-handedness of the spectacle occurring "here and now," creating—in phases[270]—the phenomenon of character and a fabularity

---

[269] See J. Alter, *A Socio-Semiotic Theory of Theatre*, Philadelphia 1990.
[270] See Z. Raszewski, *Teatr w świecie…*, 71.

approximating that of the epic but subjected to a greater, formal rigor (for instance, conic structure).

In all three of the models invoked here, the rule of the "making-present of the word" is privileged: the word—as sign (structuralists and semioticians), the word—as action (sociologists and anthropologists), the word—as expression of existence (philosophers of theater). This dependence on the word turned out in spite of everything to be the foundation—regarded from a theoretical point of view—of the theatrical convention of the twentieth century. The theater deprived of a rhetorical *raison d'être* renounced the perfection of the reflection of an image of the world for the sake of discovery (spatial-temporal) in a cycle of theatrical revolutions. Yet the record of these revolutionary conceptions continued to be perpetuated in the independently existing dramatic forms ("written on stage," as they may have been).

The dream of the return to ritual as a source of the Theater of the Future can be explained by the post-naturalistic transformation of the understanding of theater as the making-present of the play in a neo-symbolist faith in theater as the making-present of myth. In both cases it is a matter of the fabular model, independently prior to realization on stage (which is confirmed by the twentieth-century vitality of the naturalistic-symbolistic synchronism dating from the end of the nineteenth century). And also of the actuality of the utopia of perfected form inscribed in the very rule of the literary modeling of life or ritual—which took on special significance for the multimorphic, multi-version, multicultural theater of the twentieth century. "Theater would want to achieve a clarity of form as in a concelebrated Mass," wrote Zbigniew Raszewski at the end of that century. "But it would want to continually create the form itself over and over from the start."[271]

---

[271] Ibid., 150.

BEYOND UTOPIA AND FAITH:
THE SPACE OF ANTI-ILLUSION

THE DECONSTRUCTION OF REPRESENTATION: WILSON'S MODEL

The theoreticians of postmodernism were late in encompassing the theater in the orbit of their consideration, but once this occurred, they discerned almost immediately the ideal symmetry between the assumptions underlying the trend and the essence of the theatrical.[272] At once, they emphasized the active participation of theater and drama in the creation of the critical phase of modernism (especially in Europe; there was an enumeration of the examples of German expressionism, dadaism, futurism, the creativity of Maeterlinck and Yeats, and later Artaud and Brecht[273]). They went on to point out another, programmatic contiguity: every work of theater illustrates the tension between product and process (no complete final version of the work exists, after all). Finally, more than any other form of art, theater embraces the extremes of high and low culture.

In the philosophical texts of the patron saint of the entire movement, Jacques Derrida, it is no accident that the metaphor of the stage appears. The Derridian theses that the theatrical space is an undecided and at the same time deconstructive space involved in the "impossibility of unambiguity" and that "the audience becomes a stage unto itself,"[274] corresponds perfectly to the self-consciousness of twentieth-century theater and to the state of mind of the theatrology of the time. Attempts

---

[272] See S. Connor, *Postmodernist Culture: An Introduction to Theories of the Contemporary*, Oxford 1989; M. Benamou, C. Caramello (ed.), *Performance in Postmodern Culture*, Madison 1977.
[273] S. Connor, *Postmodernist Culture...*, 132.
[274] See E. and T. Sławkowie, *Teatr filozofii*, "Teatr" 1 (1988), 24.

at putting the world of drama in order after the experience of the theater of the absurd (analogous to the phenomenon of art after the end of art) also indicate the multiplicity of *mimesis* in the contemporary theater (Austin E. Quigley), the lack of dialogue and closing of the dramatic structure (John Peter), and the end of individualism and the image of "rootless existence" (George E. Wellwarth, Erika Fischer-Lichte).[275]

In 1984, Darko Suvin diagnosed the malaise of the "individualistic drama," connected with the history of the illusionistic stage.[276] In 1980, Maurice Valency announced the "end of the play" as a result of the rejection in the twentieth century of the traditional doctrine of *mimesis* and the myth of cosmic order.[277] For this reason, perhaps, the dominant theme in plays (and theater) at the end of the twentieth century seems to be the conflict between reality and illusion, between the truth of human existence and the necessary mendacity in interpersonal conventions as described by Anthony S. Abbott.[278] Precisely this conflict is intended to unite the diversity of models of post-absurdist drama: Harold Pinter, Peter Weiss, Tom Stoppard, Peter Handke.

The deconstruction of life as a stage and reality as acting can be found in such incompatible models of the theater as those of Peter Brook, Robert Wilson, Ariane Mnouchkine, Giorgio Strehler, Eugenio Barba, Tadeusz Kantor, Jerzy Grotowski, Julian Beck, and Judith Malina, etc. Kantor and Grotowski went a step farther, searching for a way out in the evocation of rituals of death and rebirth, or Grotowski and Barba, postulating the rebirth of Man with a body degraded for centuries in the culture of the West.

And yet no less important a characteristic of contemporary theater is the ubiquitous crisis since the times of the Renaissance and Baroque of the very principal of theatrical representation, combined with the

---

[275] A. E. Quigley, *The Modern Stage…*; J. Peter, *Vladimir's Carrot: Modern Drama and the Modern Imagination*, London 1987; G. E. Wellwarth, *Modern Drama and the Death of God*, Madison 1986; E. Fischer-Lichte, *Geschichte des Dramas. Epochen der Identität auf dem Theater von der Antike bis zur Gegenwart*, Tübingen 1990.

[276] D. Suvin, *To Brecht and Beyond: Soundings in Modern Dramaturgy*, Brighton 1984.

[277] M. Valency, *The End of World: An Introduction to Contemporary Drama*, Oxford 1980. See H. T. Lehmann, *Postdramatic Theatre*, London and New York 2006.

[278] A. S. Abbott, *The Vital Lie*, Tuscaloosa 1989.

The deconstruction of representation: Wilson's model

logocentric dominance of the word and faith in the rational order of things. Laying the groundwork for the rules of theatrical destruction, Derrida repeatedly evoked the intuition of Artaud, writing for instance:

> "the 'grammar' of the theater of cruelty, of which he said that it is 'to be found,' will always remain the inaccessible limit of a representation which is no repetition, of a *re*-presentation which is full presence, which does not carry its double within itself as its death, of a present which does not repeat itself, that is, of a present outside time, a non-present."[279]

These ideas have been completely domiciled in the newest theories of theater, inspired by post-modernism and deconstructionism. Richard Schechner drew attention to the principle of the directness of effect and the renunciation of any kind of semantic order (even in the understanding of Barthes's formula "density of signification")—for the sake of an order of the impossible, lasting placement of the spectacle between life and theater.[280] Robert W. Corrigan accented the rejection of the coherence of fable, characters, etc.—or any kind of re-presentation of human existence in action—in favor of presentation, autopresentation.[281]

For the semiologist Patrice Pavis, the ideal of post-modernism in the theater turns out to be the work of Robert Wilson, supplemented by the principle of the unrepeatability and impermanence of the performance, propagating the diffusion of the work's identity through its immersion in political, social, and "intercultural" contexts.[282]

The category of "anti-textuality" as a "post-Artaudian" criterion has been used in turn by Bonnie Marranca in her description of Robert Wilson's "theater of images,"[283] or the plays dating from the seventies and eighties: *A Deafman Glance* (1971); *A Letter for Queen Victoria* (1974); *Einstein on the Beach* (1976); *Death, Destruction & Detroit* (parts

---

[279] J. Derrida, *Writing and Difference*, Chicago 1978, 247–248. See E. Fuchs, *Presence and the Revenge of Writing: Re-thinking Theatre After Derrida*, "Performing Arts Journal" 2/3 (1985), 163–173.

[280] R. Schechner, *News, Sex and Performance Theory*, in: *Innovation/Renovation: New Perspectives in the Humanities*, ed. I. Hassan, S. Hassan, Madison 1983, 191.

[281] R. W. Corrigan, *The Search for New Endings: The Theatre in Search of a Fix, Part III*, "Theatre Journal" 1 (1984), 160.

[282] P. Pavis, *The Liberated Performance*, "Modern Drama" 1 (1982), 62. See K. Arens, *Robert Wilson: Is Postmodern Performance Possible?*, "Theatre Journal" 1 (1991), 14–39.

[283] B. Marranca (ed.), *The Theatre of Images*, New York 1996.

BEYOND UTOPIA AND FAITH: THE SPACE OF ANTI-ILLUSION

I and II, 1979 and 1987); and *CIVIL WarS* (1983–1984). Much talked about at the end of the twentieth century, this artist, who in his time studied architecture, created, in Marranca's opinion, living pictures on the stage (recalling the "stage compositions" of Kandinsky)—or rather "a landscape of sculptured forms lit by the power of brilliant colors."[284] The result is a flattening of the onstage image and, following contemporary painting, a reliance on the extra-temporal presentation of abstraction.

In the Wilsonian "theater of pictures," however, Marranca noticed above all a contemporary implementation of the Wagnerian idea of the *Gesamtkunstwerk*—owing to what she regarded as "unifying all the arts in a spiritual atmosphere of illusion and mysticism," thanks to which it was possible to "lead his audience into what Wagner called 'a spiritualized state of clairvoyance.'"[285] Clearly visible in the choice of these formulations is the distinct influence of Artaud, more so than that of German romanticism (although in an important way Marranca completes the list, functioning in Germany, of contemporary Wagnerians[286]).

Both the community of art and opera-ness nevertheless find particular expression in Wilson. And so the arias take on the form of auditory declamations, the function of the *leitmotiv* is taken over by the recurring visual themes (in place of the absent plot); while the construction of the whole is determined by rules that are rather architectonic than musical.

A further trait of this theatrical reality is syncretism. Of Wilson, after all, Marranca states: "From the Dadaist-Futurist-Surrealist past he has absorbed the belief in the value of simultaneous experience."[287] In the range of subjects taken up by Wilson: "human interaction, murder, the Civil War, justice, ecology, pilots and a plane crash, cultural imperialism, ancient civilizations and the atom bomb"—Marranca notices an ideology-free (!) allusion to the romantic utopia of purifying the cruel, unjust world and returning to the "paradisaical existence" of the New Society.[288]

---

[284] Ibid., 44.

[285] Ibid., 39.

[286] See G. Förg (ed.), *Unsere Wagner: Joseph Beuys, Heinrich Müller, Karlheinz Stockausen, Hans-Jürgen Syberberg. Essays*, Frankfurt/M 1984.

[287] B. Marranca (ed.), *The Theatre of Images*, 40.

[288] Ibid.

The deconstruction of representation: Wilson's model

Supposedly a manifestation of this attitude is the active participation in work on the play and in its production of Christopher Knowles, a teenager suffering from autism, representing "pre-consciousness, innocence and futurity" or—in Jungian terminology—the "child archetype," not as a "theatrical" symbol, but as its (real) actualization.[289]

This, at least, is how Marranca interprets the naturalness and strangeness that Knowles brought to the stage owing to his ever-so-real dysfunction. The phenomenology of autism turned out to be the anchor for this theater: the remaining actors imitated Knowles, rather than the other way around.[290] During the entr'actes played by Wilson and Knowles (as recapitulations of previous events or foreshadowings of future ones in the play) the principle was the adoption of behaviors typical of autistic children (repetition, echolalia, puns, and imitation)—in a structure of two rhythms of playing with blocks (of letters, syllables, expressions…).[291]

Marranca states that Wilson treated the myths of American culture the same way (on a suggestion from Knowles, Wilson introduced, as one of the themes in his production, the mythical Wild West character known as the Sundance Kid in "a long verbal aria that builds from the rhythm of a single line, 'THE SUNDANCE KID IS BEAUTIFUL.'"[292] Fragments of banal colloquial conversations, and quotations from the press, television, and film appear in the production as *ready-made*, all of them stripped of their meaning and used because of the phonetic quality of the quotations.

The architectonic form of *A Letter for Queen Victoria* is built on diverse variants of the application of the numbers 4, 3, and 2. There are four acts, a string quartet plays throughout, two dancers dance without interruption on the lower catwalk. The actors are numbered (from 1 to 4), while the symbolism of the images is frequently based on bipolar contrasts:

> "Black and white, light and dark symbolize consciousness and the unconscious, knowledge and lack of knowledge—states of being that Wilson explores

---

[289] Ibid.
[290] Ibid., 44.
[291] Ibid., 43.
[292] Ibid., 41.

thematically"[293] (from the social point of view, in Marranca's opinion, "black and white" may also be related to the subject of racism and justice).

"I was thinking about the number four—the four acts, the string quartet and the four characters," wrote Robert Wilson. "They sound like four different people yet they all sound the same. I never had to explain anything to Christopher because he'd just take what I was doing and use it for his own purposes. When I started numbering people in the script—character 1, character 2, character 3, and character 4—he picked up on it and did the same thing."[294]

As in other plays by Wilson, the development of action in *A Letter to Queen Victoria* is based on the Dadaistic principles of transformation and chance. Each act begins with a "tableau" to which the people are gradually "added." The numbered actors take up and discard various "roles" (or rather verbal actions without reason or continuation). Various objects (a vat, a rock, a salad, a crocodile), with no theatrical function or connection with what is happening on stage, appear.[295]

Marranca refers to Wilson's work as "theater as assemblage art."[296] In her opinion, Wilson—like every deconstructionist—refuses to accept "the absolutism of language." Excluded from its normal contexts and deprived of the stability of significant structures, the word functions as an element of the poetics of sounds (utilizing the principle of insistent repetition). These are, as Arthur Holmberg wrote, "words arranged not in terms of semantics or syntax but in autistic patterns that heightened their materiality—how they sound, how they look."[297]

The use of language, and in general the whole auditory sphere in the production, are based on the aesthetics of dissonance (the performance begins and ends with a loud scream). Aside from "scream songs, grunts and shrieks," there are specially invented words like SPUPS, PIRUP, HAP and HATH… In short—words liberated from semantics and the logic of syntax. There are also pure sounds: shots from a pistol, bombs going off, the clatter of horses' hooves, train whistles. The effect of all this is

---

[293] Ibid.
[294] R. Wilson, *Preface*, in: *The Theatre of Images*, ed. B. Marranca, New York 1996, 48.
[295] B. Marranca (ed.), *The Theatre of Images*, 39.
[296] Ibid.
[297] A. Holmberg, *The Theatre of Robert Wilson*, Cambridge 1996, 46.

INTRODUCTION
1
2
3
4

ACT I

1	1	1	1
2	2	2	2
PILOTS	PILOTS	GUARD	1A
	BILLY		2A
			BILLY
			CHRIS
			PILOT

ACT II

1	1	1	1
2	2	2	2
3	3	3	3
4	4	4	4
GUARD	GUARD	CIVIL WAR SOLDIER	CHRIS
	CHRIS	JIM	

ACT III

	1C		1B	
1D		1E		1A
2D	2C	2E	2B	2A

ACT IV

1	1	1	1
2	2	2	2
2A	2A	2A	PILOTS
3	3	3	
4	4	4	
BILLY	BILLY	BILLY	
		CHRIS	

Figure 10. Robert Wilson: The architectonic form of *A Letter to Queen Victoria**

---

* B. Marranca (ed.), *The Theatre of Images*, 51–52.

BEYOND UTOPIA AND FAITH: THE SPACE OF ANTI-ILLUSION

"a sound collage made from the juxtaposition of numerous textures and rhythms of sounds"—free of any kind of meaning, in the semantic sense.[298]

The Dadaistic principle of collage also dominates the visual sphere of the performance, creating "a new world where objects, movements, attitudes and gestures form a vocabulary of a visual language which replaces the verbal one ... a world of narrative images which transcend materiality"[299] (as in Artaudian "anarchic dissociation"?). Marranca goes even farther, calling *A Letter to Queen Victoria* "an exercise in the sharpness of sense perception."[300]

While conversation is lacking, "the actors speak in sentences which, like echoes, are transmitted from one act to another."[301] Given the lack of communication, discourse appears as something completely irrational, while the mechanical nature of repetition (like the stroboscopic Chitter-Chatter sequence), in combination with the same gestures, makes it possible to create a new kind of musicality, or an operatic quality as Wilson himself would have it. Marranca describes the result as "a prelinguistic world" (as proposed by Artaud and Derrida), where sounds and gestures have the power to create "a new grammar of human interaction."[302]

> "I called *A Letter For Queen Victoria* an 'opera,'" wrote Robert Wilson, "because everything in it happens at once, the way it does in operas and the way it does in life."[303]

If the construction of Wilson's *Letter to Queen Victoria* can indeed be compared to the Wagnerian *Gesamtkunstwerk*, the message itself can be placed only in a cultural context in which all boundaries of internal order have been effaced and all orientation points and opportunities for logical accumulation removed.

---

[298] B. Marranca (ed.), *The Theatre of Images*, 41.
[299] Ibid.
[300] Ibid., 42.
[301] Ibid.
[302] Ibid., 43.
[303] Ibid., 49.

THE DESEMANTICIZATION OF THE MESSAGE: KANTOR'S MODEL

Henri Gouhier's definition "Représenter c'est rendre présent par des présences" (to represent is to make something present through presences)[304] is totally inadequate to Tadeusz Kantor's Theater of Death, the essence of which—as described in detail elsewhere[305]—is precisely the "impossibility of making present" both the dead "literary pre-existence" of the spectacle (drama, fable, characters) and the subjective memory of what-was.

Neither does the semiologists' definition "theater is the spatialization of literature"[306] fit the assumptions of Kantor, who used linguistic citations from Witkiewicz's *Tumor Brainowicz*, visual references to Gombrowicz's *Ferdydurke* and the prose of Schulz in *The Dead Class* to create possibilities (even for an instant) of the ostentatiously "substitute" existence of the dead pupils in moments when the class came to life and the photograph of memory dissolved. This is one of the principles of the Theater of Death: literary roles and motifs make impossible the rebirth (in reconstructed reminiscences of long-dead characters and incidents), or rather such reconstruction is lost in the trap of "impersonation." Inaugurated with the 1956 *Cuttlefish*, the years-long "playing (with) Witkacy" in the Cricot 2 theater, extending through *The Dead Class* of 1975, was based on the assumption that the plays—even the most avant-garde ones that nevertheless had long been fulfilled in the imagination of their author, constituted "the DEAD world of the

---

[304] H. Gouhier, *L'Essence du théâtre*, 15–20.
[305] See K. Pleśniarowicz, *The Dead Memory Machine: Tadeusz Kantor's Theatre of Death*, trans. W. Brand, Aberystwyth 2004.
[306] T. Kowzan, *Teatr jako uprzestrzennienie...*

DEAD."[307] For Kantor, the fundamental contradiction of the theater is found in the stage—play relationship, and even the momentary unity of literature and theater is impossible. On the one side of this eternal conflict there is, thus, the fiction of the play, its fable, and the "reality of fictional drama,"[308] associated with the condition of death. The reality of the theater, entangled in the conflict with theatrical illusion, remains on the other side. The stage is the place where this transformation of the eternal condition of death into the condition of momentary, ostensible, simulated life plays out.

It is not, after all, literature that undergoes "spatialization" here, but rather the photographic plates of memory of Kantor himself as he creates the Theater of Death by conjuring up the metaphysics of photography. The black-and-white image of the small group of pupils sitting at their desks constantly returns in performances of *The Dead Class* and freezes into immobility. The attempts at theatrical action undertaken by the actors dissolves this freeze-frame into a helpless confusion of supererogatory words and futile gestures, and then after a certain time everything re-freezes again into that initial image from the past which, at a sign from Kantor, again dissolves.

Another crucial semantic rhythm inheres in this: dying (in the starting-point photographic plate of memory) and coming to life (in attempts at substitute theatrical action)—the rhythm of coming to life and dying. In any case, it betokens only momentary existence, ostensible and futile, in strictly delineated boundaries (watched over by Death, the classroom cleaning woman, who intervenes ruthlessly). In turn, the rhythm of alternating concentration and dissolution permeates the covert or overt allusions to historical time, although in the end there is no way to determine whether the photographic plates from the First World War or those evoking the Holocaust era are dominant. All the more so because attempts at making present the shattered historical consciousness—the "Historical Hallucinations" or the "fragments from the Bible, Mythology and History in the form of school answers"[309]—fail

---

[307] T. Kantor, *Miejsce teatralne*, in: idem, *Wielopole, Wielopole...*, Kraków 1984, 130.
[308] Kantor interviewed by Borowski, in: W. Borowski, *Kantor*, Warszawa 1982, 51–52.
[309] Kantor interviewed by R. de Monticelli, *Sulla scena pasasano fantasmi d'avanguardia*, "Corriere della Sera" (January 29, 1978).

to create a true Yesterday, to reconstruct a Whole. What they do achieve is to keep provoking the pupils to discover their sensuous corporeality, mutual aggression, and cruelty.

On the other hand, the main idea of the play can be embraced in the formula of the Impossible Return to a dead past of which the only vestiges are accidental and worn-out Memory Photographs. The performance is conducted directly by Kantor himself, who intervenes in the course of the action, makes remarks to the actors, and personally sets up and dissolves the Photographs of Dead Memory. With a gesture of his hand he introduces the rhythm of an old sentimental waltz playing from a gramophone, bringing back to life "the charm of old memories," and regulates the intensity of the hollow clunking of balls in the Cradle-Coffin. The photographic plates from the past are the only true reality for the artist who manipulates them and also for the entire play, subject to the compulsion of avant-garde utopia or the continually renewed inauguration of revolutionary development toward a new future. In Kantor's opinion, "Life can be expressed in art only by the absence of life, by an appeal to death,"[310] absence attests to presence, and the essence of existence is pretense, deprivation, and incompletion.

In the Theater of Death there is no fable or causal line of action. There is, on the other hand, a sort of rhythm of passage from the dead, motionless time of the "school" photographs to the series of images which, like film, offer a delusive promise of continuation in the future. The moving photographs return in a set order created by image and sound in conjunction: the Parades of the dead pupils around the schoolroom desks as well as their slow rising behind the desks are accompanied by the sentimental, old-fashioned *François* waltz; there are successive lessons (where the teacher calls on one of the students), the keening Jewish prayers, and the voices from the school's past playing from the loudspeaker. There are six of these memory photographs, the dominants of dead memory:

1. The photograph ("Illusion") of the dead class: the pupils or their dummies sit at their desks (or the desks are empty);

---

[310] K. Miklaszewski, *Encounters With Tadeusz Kantor*, London and New York 2002, 39.

BEYOND UTOPIA AND FAITH: THE SPACE OF ANTI-ILLUSION

2. The "Parade" of the pupils around the desks to the rhythm of the waltz *François*;
3. The succeeding "Lessons" around thematic slogans (for example "King David," "Prometheus," "ear," or "finger," or "school" activities connected with the metaphor of sleep ("Night Lessons") or death "Too Long in All Souls Day";
4. The school transforms itself into a "Cheder": the actors raise their hands and rock back and forth rhythmically in the ecstasy of Jewish prayer;
5. "The Grand Toasts": the pupils repeatedly rise up and freeze at their desks, transfixed by the sounds of the waltz *François*;
6. Auditory sound bites of memory called "Historical Hallucinations"—these are slivers of school learning, such as "*Hannibal ante portas!, The Ides of March!, Galia est omnis divisa!*" and so on.

Aside from the six repeatedly recurring photographic plates of dead memory, there exists in the performance a separate cycle of six isolated fragments of action based on "playing with literature" or evoking stories that momentarily free themselves from the limitations imposed by the memory photographs. But even then it is not the pupils, called at best to the existence of some other, who dominate, but rather the Cleaning Woman/Death who rules over them. The surrogate life outside the memory photographs, in these "autonomous segments," never in fact lasts long and has no direct continuation.

Liberation from the circle of successively evoked photographic plates of memory can be called a progression that, of course, opposes the regression of the inevitable return to the memory photographs after the exhaustion of the effort at maintaining the theater, "playing (with) Witkacy," or after the next triumphant action by the Cleaning Woman/Death. The important thing in the progressive-regressive rhythm is the very act of violating and restoring equilibrium, the unending contention between the rescuing of unity and the temptation of change. Thus the symmetry of the six photographic memory plates and the six autonomous sequences:

1. "The 'Games' played by the Cleaning Woman" ("hunting down trash," the futile stacking of dusty books, the reading of old newspapers) and the Imperial-Royal anthem sung by the Beadle;

2. "The Family Machine' along with the 'Mechanical Cradle,'" or the death-birth scene with quotations from Witkacy (Act I of *Tumor Brainowicz*), concluding with the "Great Spring Cleaning": "the deathly mowing down" of all the old people by the Cleaning Woman;
3. "The Secret Official Executioner in the WC" (the "oration" by the Old Man/Doppelganger, consisting of "intricate explanations" and supervised by the Cleaning Woman);
4. "Collusions with the Void": a series of mutual acts of aggression—the "murder" of the pupils in turn as they leave the classroom. Allusions to previously transcended memory photographs appear. The elaborated finale of this sequence is the battle between the Cleaning Woman and the Old People/Doppelgangers;
5. The "Simultaneous Orgy" and the "Colonial Robinsonial": images and actions inspired by fragments of Act II of *Tumor Brainowicz*;
6. The Woman with a Mechanical Cradle, singing a Jewish lullaby while sitting on a pile of trash next to the cradle/coffin, after which comes the "Dummy Dialogue" which uses introductory excerpts from *Tumor Brainowicz*. This sequence is the introduction to the climactic "Theater of the Automata." At this point, the Old People are imprisoned in continually repeating gestures, while the Cleaning Woman sets about the "corpse washing."

To rescue this symmetry, so that the metaphorical sense is not completely subordinated to the apparent existence of the dead pupils, so that the growing influence of Witkacy does not turn into "normal" theater, Kantor definitively stops the spinning of the spiral of activity in a cycle of freeze-frames from the "Theater of the Automata."

It is precisely the spiral that seems to be the most adequate graphic model for the development of the theme of impossible memory in Kantor's Theater of Death. Such a visual schematization represents a temptation to apply a musical analysis of the work according to Charles Mauron's definition as a search for obsessive themes and the investigation of their variations.[311] It is possible to identify elements of the subconscious amidst the manipulation of images and themes. In *The Dead Class*, however, the composition of comparable elements (the memory photographs) and contrasting elements (the autonomous sequences) makes visible precisely the impossibility of consciously reconstructing the unconscious. Every explanation of the predominant idea behind the performance, including psychoanalytic explanations, falls into the trap of unambiguity—and misses the most important thing: the "Collusions with the Void" of the title, the game being played between illusion and reality (as Kantor liked to say) or—as it might be reformulated—between semanticization and desemanticization, the simultaneous bestowal and cancellation of meanings. The spiral shape of *The Dead Class* evokes limitless domains of tradition. The imaging of the spiral/labyrinth often serves to present the journey "into the depths"—of the past, the unconscious, and death.

The spiral, furthermore, makes it possible to grasp the rules of the artist's theatrical procedure, especially the rhythms of progression and regression, according to a more or less permanent arrangement of certain repeatable situations or images which seem again and again to come up and be passed over in an established sequence as the cycle turns. The nearer the end of the performance (and the center of the spiral), the more they become gradually fading echoes, which distinctly suggests the winding-in of the spiral rather than its infinite expansion. Its leftward movement agrees with the direction of all the "Parades" of the dead pupils around the benches, as in the symbolism of a dream.[312]

Similarly, the classroom as a whole follows a different, metaphorical rhythm: similarity and differentiation. In the photographic plates of dead memory, the pupils melt into a homogenous class mechanism; the uniformity of their black, funereal suits and the corpselike paleness of their faces then become dominant. Kantor states that this was "a blatant example of the bio-object" in which the "desks and the pupils constituted a single organism."[313] But this immobile image instantly dissolves and

---

[311] C. Mauron, *Des métaphores obsédantes au mythe personnel. Introduction á la psychocritique*, Paris 1963.

[312] See M. L. von Franz, *The Process of Individuation*, in: *Man and His Symbols*, ed. C. G. Jung, London 1979, 225–227.

[313] T. Kantor, *Miejsce teatralne*, 138–139.

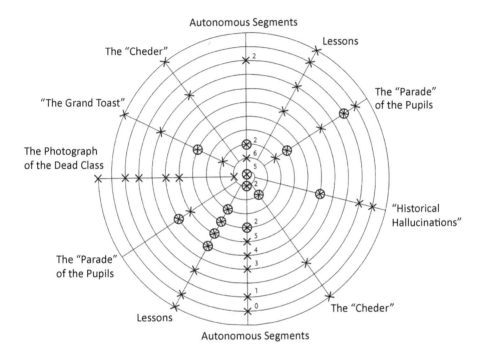

Figure 11. K. Pleśniarowicz: The Spiral of Return in Kantor's "The Dead Class"*

---

* K. Pleśniarowicz, *The Dead Memory Machine...*, 207.

the memory machine compels the Old People to come out with the schoolboy showing off from the "Lesson" and the games with superfluous literature, although these individual reflexes are mercilessly suppressed by the other members of the classroom community (regardless of the inevitable intervention by the Cleaning Woman).

The rhythm of similarity and differentiation—the guiding principle for the presentation of the pupils of the dead class—is also carried over into the way the action develops. This is connected with the avant-garde foundations of *The Dead Class*; the principles of montage (or "organized disorder") and the accidental ("surprises") were obligatory in Kantor's works. Montage and the accidental are according to Peter Bürger, elementary categories in the description of avant-garde works of art.[314] The successively dissolving photographic plates of dead memory, as well as the autonomous sequences stricken by the making-present of the impossible, summon up an impression of a system of accidentally juxtaposed situations, pictures, and shreds of actions and thought—and it is never known what they will lead to or how they will end. The only thing that seems to be inevitable is the recursion of the photographic plates and the association with what already was, and especially the return to the frozen class in the introductory photograph. And yet it still remains a surprise—which photographic plate (in its entirety or in the form of an "echo") will reappear at precisely the moment when the return to the "Illusion" occurs?

In the face of impossible subjects (dead memories, absent history, superfluous literature), in the face of the impossibility of making present any kind of fable, the individual ingredients of the performance combine in formal metonymic (contiguity) and metaphorical (similarity) relations. Relations of the first type arise *in praesentia*, in the linear development of the performance where non-identical situations and images are directly adjacent: various photographic plates of dead memory and isolated phases of autonomous sequences. Relations of the second type exist *in absentia*, in the potential memory of the beholders who recognize the metaphorical similarities of even distant images and situations.

---

[314] See P. Bürger, *Theory of the Avant-Garde*, Manchester 1984, 66, 72.

The desemanticization of the message: Kantor's model

The recursiveness of themes, images, and motives that are characteristic of Kantor's Theater of Death counteracts the differentiation so inextricably linked with that theater, undermining the significances set in motion in the insistence of repetition. It turns out in the end that the added senses, the background significances, are invalidated by excess—in a refined process of not arriving at semantic discipline, logical rigor, or structural order—in the rhythm of bestowing and losing significances.

In accordance with the Idea of Transgression, the complex of cognitive postulates formulated by Kantor in regard to art—the nearer the "zero point," the nearer the truth. Life, and more precisely all aspects of human existence, human consciousness, are best expressed through their absence. Things are analogous with the grammar of the theater used in *The Dead Class*: the procedural rules of the theatrical ritual turn out to be more important than the meaning.

The first of these complexes of rules is connected with the already mentioned impossibility of making memory, history, and literature present. The constant proofs of this in refined semantic rhythms of progress and regression, concentration and distraction, invocation and annulment, are more important than the real vestiges that can be sought of the memory of a class in a Galician Imperial and Royal *gimnasium* in 1914, of the fate of the Jews of Central Europe, of the literary or artistic inspirations of the performance.

The second complex of rules is inscribed in the means of playing with significances: metonymous realities and the alternation, repetition, and metamorphoses within the confines of metaphorical series. And also in the realization of those means within the framework of rhythms of objectification and de-objectification, similarity and differentiation. A direct analogy with grammar inheres in the repeated application of these same, recurring rules in the Theater of Death. The climactic "Theater of the Automata" shows precisely that according to these rules the performance could be prolonged unendingly. The incidents in the performance are not, after all, part of a continuum of cause and effect. Vestiges of these connections exist in the autonomous sequences and constitute a fabular borrowing from Witkacy. The succession of incidents is motivated by these quasi-grammatical and rhetorical principles (and the semantic rhythms that result from them).

BEYOND UTOPIA AND FAITH: THE SPACE OF ANTI-ILLUSION

In his "playing (with) Witkacy," Kantor breaks associations of a causal type in theatrical action, implementing now the one and now the other of two extreme tendencies:
1. bringing about the chaotic, excessive differentiation of elements;
2. leaving these elements in a uniform, homogeneous, internally disorganized configuration.

Serving as an example of the first tendency is *Kurka Wodna* [The Water Hen], and even more so *Nadobnisie i koczkodany* [*Dainty Shapes and Hairy Apes* or *Lovelies and Dowdies*], in which there is a deliberate assumption of the impossibility of taking in all the elements of the performance from the position of the beholder. An example of the second tendency is not so much the entire performance as theoretically conceived situations (and attempts at their implementation), when the actors were supposed to be deprived of the possibility of acting by being enmeshed in a configuration characterized by uniformity, homogeneity, a lack of organization, and so on—and also a lack of relevant causes and a final, logical goal. For example, the noisy, mobile *Maszyna z krzeseł (Aneantyzacyjna)* [The Machine of Annihilation], that drowns out and jostles the actors speaking their parts in *Wariat i zakonnica* [The Madman and The Nun]; the actors crushed and mingled with sacks in a wardrobe in a situation whose dialogue is borrowed from the play *W małym dworku* [The Country House], etc.

Not once does *The Dead Class* fall into the extremes of chaos or repetitiveness, although both forces are present in the play. They create a quasi-musical rule for the organization of the play, based on contrast and comparison, which is something new in the history of Cricot 2. The consistent destruction of cause-and-affect connections in theatrical action (the demolition of fiction, and at the same time of the semantic message), the destruction of relations of the illustrative type between theater and the "pre-existing" play or subject (the breakdown of the principle of representation) bore fruit in the form of a multilayered configuration of games centered around significances. In this configuration the overriding rhythm of semanticization and desemanticization is made up of elementary rhythms connected with the impossible making present of three themes: dead memory (the rhythm of coming to life and dying]), superfluous literature (the rhythm of summoning up and canceling out), absent history (the rhythm of alternating concentration and dissolution). This overriding rhythm is present in each of the plans for "ostensible symbolism" (the spiral of return [the rhythm of progression and regression]); the poles of memory [the rhythm of similarity and differentiation]); models of aphasia—the rhythm of continuation and contradiction. The linguistic behavior of the pupils in the dead class represents almost all the symptoms noted by Jakobson in cases of aphasia, in terms of similarity (faults in selection and substitution) and in contiguity (reduced skill in combination and contexture).[315] This kind of destruction transformed itself into its opposite: into construction.

Kantor's performance has a quite refined construction with many rhythms built in: aural and visual, semantic and emotional. The rules of the rhythmic repeatability of the sequences of sounds and spatial images recall the principles of "visual musicality." Attempts at just such a description of the structure of the *Dead Class* approach most closely, it seems, the mystery of the masterpiece and its worldwide triumph.

Balancing between the avant-garde ideal of pure abstraction and the unavoidable conventionalization of all artistic action means the negation of all semantic (illusionistic) references external to the performance. In the Theater of Death everything that fits Kantor's definition of "pre-existence" (such as impossible memory, absent history, superfluous literature), but also post-existence, or the making present of what is dead, in the process of reception, and later, in commentaries and interpretation, must be annulled.

---

[315] R. Jakobson, *Two Aspects of Language and Two Type of Aphasic Disturbance*, in: R. Jakobson, M. Halle, *Fundamentals of Language*, The Hague 1956, 57.

THE DELIMITATION OF CULTURE: BROOK'S MODEL

In the well-known book *The Empty Space*, Peter Brook carried out his familiar division into Deadly, Holy, Rough and Immediate theaters.[316] The Holy theater was an expression of the dream, frequent in the 1960s and 1970s, of the rebirth of authentic links between the modern stage and ritual and myth. In the footsteps of Artaud, there was a proposal at the time that the Invisible should again become the Visible, that the Eternal would find expression in rhythms, forms, and gestures, that the stage would meet all the criteria of the *locus sacer*, and time would take on the ritual dimension of sameness, presentation, and presence.

In much of his mature theatrical activity, Brook appeals directly to myth and ritual—in the whole cycle of well-known productions, after leaving the Royal Shakespeare Company, including *Orghast* (1971), *The Iks* (1975); and *Conference of the Birds* (1976). Sometimes he plucked fabular material out of mythical stories, or resorted to the fruitful theatricality of patterns of religious activity. Elsewhere he gave proof of his faith in the supremacy of the ideas of co-participation and community. The most famous manifestation of this attitude was of course his *Mahabharata*. Brook produced several versions of the *Mahabharata* with different lineups of actors: the French-language version had its premiere as part of the Avignon Festival on July 7, 1985; the English-language version was shown for the first time in Zurich in August 1987, and finally the film version was produced in 1990.

This legendary production has repeatedly been described as the logical crowning of Brook's many years of creative process, in search of what

---

[316] P. Brook, *The Empty Space: The Theatre Today*, London 1968.

he called "interior culture." But it was also a personal illustration of the "intercultural" principles he adopted, a practical lesson in the theses of the anthropology of the theater which were obligatory in the work of the International Centre for Theatrical Research (Centre International de Recherche Théâtrale) that Brook directed in Paris from 1971 on.

In the *Mahabharata*, Peter Brook utilized the experience of the Paris Centre—conceived of as a place for the meeting of many cultures—but also his research trips with an international group of actors to Iran, Africa, the USA, and India. This led to the gathering of what would seem to be a wealth of incompatible experience. In the *Mahabharata* Brook could simultaneously summon up, in the words of Margaret Croyden, "ritual theater, Oriental storytelling, Indian classical theater, magic and clowning, the broad scope of epic staging, the tone and timbre of Shakespearean tragedy and the savagery of the theater of cruelty."[317]

Like Barba or Grotowski, Brook led a search for the universal theater on the fundamental level: the body and voice of the actor. The quest for universal human and cultural competence in the ancient Indian epic (which remains a living source at all cultural levels throughout the whole South Asian region) struck Irving Wardle as being in accord with Ottomar Krejči's thesis that the theater can encompass the contemporary world only by fleeing from it—and creating bygone narratives anew.[318] Brook's *Mahabharata* was thus an attempt at connecting fragmentary contemporary experience with the lost, mythical image of the Whole, an attempt at a renewed, living association of real life with the authentic, primeval unity with ritual that had been lost in the West.

This is one of the possible answers to the question: Why did Brook choose the *Mahabharata*? Another seems to be the centuries-old and still vital primal theatrical forms of the East—since the phenomenon has no counterpart in the West, Brook's universal version could fill that gap in a certain sense. It is also possible to argue that the *Mahabharata* is a "complete eternal cosmic history of mankind" expressed in one work,

---

[317] M. Croyden, *Peter Brook Transforms an Indian Epic for the Stage*, "The New York Times" (August 25, 1985).

[318] I. Wardle, *Brook and Shakespeare* quoted by D. Williams, *Theatre of Innocence and of Experience: Peter Brook's International Centre: An Introduction*, in: *Peter Brook and "The Mahabharata": Critical Perspectives*, ed. idem, London 1990, 22.

a phenomenon unknown in Europe where cosmic history had existed only in fragmentary versions scattered in various masterpieces.

According to Margaret Croyden: "Revered in India but little known in the West, the *Mahabharata* is to South Asia what the Bible along with the Iliad and the Odyssey are to us."[319] Thus Brook was tempted to create a western synthesis according to an existing pattern "borrowed" from the heritage of the East (for example, he introduced the western conception of fate to his *Mahabharata*)—this was one of the many charges that natives of India brought against the production.[320] Rustom Bharucha wrote about "one of the most blatant (and accomplished) appropriations of Indian culture," claiming that Brook "decontextualized it from its history in order to 'sell' it to audiences in the West."[321]

One of the stages in the preparations for the production was a trip to India by the whole troupe. The Pole Andrzej Seweryn was a participant and reported that:

> "Once we had come together as a group, we were given specific tasks to fulfill. On one occasion, at the temple in the forest, Peter asked us all to go into the woods and to bring something back. Some people gathered leaves, others found dry branches and flowers. I brought back a handful of earth. We put all this material in one corner, then began to work on an exercise with our eyes closed. While I was involved in this, I suddenly became aware of a strange presence. Opening one eye, I saw an Indian woman approach the little altar we had built: she knelt in front of it, prayed and then left. For me, that was one of the most remarkable moments of the entire journey. Quite simply it had proved to us that God is everywhere."[322]

Aside from experiencing the ubiquity of the *sacrum* and participation in the living ritual of *Mudiattu*, one of the things that the troupe remembered was the important role of the three elements of earth, water, and fire. These elements were also the three main components of the stage design for the production of the *Mahabharata*.

---

[319] M. Croyden, *Peter Brook Transforms...*

[320] See G. Dasgupta, *"The Mahabharata": Peter Brook's Orientalism*, in: *Interculturalism and Performance: Writings from PAJ [Performing Arts Journal]*, ed. B. Marranca, G. Dasgupta, New York 1991, 75–82.

[321] R. Bharucha, *Theatre and the World: Performance and the Politics of Culture*, London 1993, 68.

[322] A. Seweryn interviewed by M. Millon, in: *Peter Brook and "The Mahabharata"...*, 88–89.

The delimitation of culture: Brook's model

Brook's program had nothing in common with ethnological imitation. It was rather a search for whatever people from the West could relate to in the epic, what they would be capable of understanding. The author of the script, Jean Claude Carrière, admitted that "nearly half of the scenes in the play do not appear in the original." Furthermore, "the secondary stories ... which are those the characters tell among themselves" were omitted, and traits of some omitted characters were incorporated in the creation of the sixteen characters in the play.[323] Above all, Carrière and Brook constructed a linear plot for the story as a whole, despite the fact that, as Rustom Bharucha put it, "Nothing could be more foreign to the *Mahabharata* than linearity."[324]

The Indian nature of the play was firmly discarded through the use of several interpretive filters that made it possible to reconstruct the epic (limited to a closed culture) as a form of drama: open, epic, and universal. In sum, taking account of the Western optics—which led to accusations of a British and imperial, or neocolonial and patriarchal attitude to India that was formulated not only by Indians—Brook defended himself by saying that the *Mahabharata*, as a *liber mundi*, was the property of all mankind, and not only India (on the same principle, after all, a classical Kathakali troupe staged Indian adaptations of *The Iliad* and *King Lear* in those years).[325]

The *Mahabharata* presents a dynastic conflict between two rival groups of cousins, the Pandavas and the Kauravas, which ends catastrophically. "It is a basic decline-and-fall story of rival family factions destroying the very universe that is their inheritance." As opposed to the Western concept of fate, however, as Michael Billington states, "moral blame is never apportioned, words like sin and evil are never used and the great god Krishna foresees and laments the coming holocaust but seems powerless to prevent it."[326]

Despite the role of myth, the production had little in common with ritual. Brook deliberately avoided preconceptions about Hindu culture out of a correct belief that an insincere presentation of them would mar

---

[323] G. O'Connor, *The Mahabharata: Peter Brook's Epic in the Making*, London 1989, 59.
[324] R. Bharucha, *Theatre and the World...*, 75.
[325] D. Williams, *Theatre of Innocence...*, 24–25.
[326] M. Billington, *Krishna Comes to the City of the Popes*, "The Guardian" (July 16, 1983).

the aim of the production, which was to be a revelation of timeless verities according to the rule "do not imitate, but express" (a "taste of India," and not the symbolism of Hindu philosophy[327]). Brook further believed that "cooperation with performers of sixteen nationalities makes it possible to exhibit a theme that goes beyond any one, concrete culture."

In practice, this universalism depended on a joining of the traditions of East and West thanks to the introduction of interpretive frames derived from Shakespeare (which in the case of Peter Brook, famous producer of *A Midsummer Night's Dream*, seems completely to be expected). It was none other than Shakespeare who was intended to guarantee the efficacy of the mechanism of universalization, while at the same time being the most accessible instrument of the multicultural in the staging of the *Mahabharata*. Theatrology even thought up an appropriate semiotic term for defining the inter-cultural production, in practice combining elements of one's own and alien cultures: "*cultural transformation.*"[328] A side effect of the Shakespearization of the *Mahabharata* was the inscribing in the production of not only the Western concept of fate, but also the Western structures of the hero and of time.

Brook proved an analogy between the two greatest theatrical traditions of the East and West, finding in the *Mahabharata* "the extraordinary quality of Shakespeare," saying "I think *The Mahabharata* is Shakespearean."[329] He proved that Arjuna or Karna are as familiar to contemporary Hindus, living characters, like Falstaff or Hamlet for Europeans. That the *Mahabharata*, like the entire works of Shakespeare, is a closed, cosmic world "where everything exists—except the author."[330]

Despite the suggested similarity of the two closed worlds, Brook decided to introduce a mythical narrator unknown to Shakespeare—Vyasa—into his version of the Indian story of mankind, seeing in it

---

[327] P. Brook, *The Presence of India: An Introduction*, in: *Peter Brook and "The Mahabharata": Critical Perspectives*, ed. D. Williams, London 1990, 43.

[328] See E. Fischer-Lichte, *Staging the Foreign as Cultural Transformation*, in: *The Dramatic Touch of Difference, Theatre, Own and Foreign*, ed. E. Fischer-Lichte, M. Gissenwehrer, J. Riley, Tübingen 1990, 277–287.

[329] Brook interviewed by D. Britton, *Theater, Popular and Special, and the Perils of Cultural Piracy*, in: *Peter Brook and "The Mahabharata": Critical Perspectives*, ed. D. Williams, London 1990, 57.

[330] Brook interviewed by Marie-Hélène Estienne, "Théâtre en Europe" 7 (1985).

The delimitation of culture: Brook's model

"a realistic relationship to the story." Vyasa tells the whole story to the child accompanying him, the copyists, and the spectators (the fact that it is precisely a child who accompanies "an impressive old guru" is regarded by Brook as "more touching").[331]

Furthermore, the procedure of the interculturization and graduated epicization of the play (precisely here an analogy was found with Brecht and his "distancing without distance"[332]) ultimately prevailed over the idea of reading the *Mahabharata* as a cosmic work—in an analogy to Shakespeare (which perhaps would have more fully expressed the idea of the intercultural).

According to Patrice Pavis, "an imaginary India" from Brook's production represented at most "a taste of India" ("it has all the flavor of India")—"India is suggested by the beaten earth, the sea-green water, the fires lit to attract the protection of the gods; it is both the real earth of the Indian subcontinent and the symbolic terrain of humanity as a whole." Furthermore, "the references to the source culture are easily understood by the audience because universal transcultural factors have been considered."[333]

It seems that, as has not been sufficiently appreciated in the extensive literature on the subject, the tactic of the universalization of the Indian epic was an appeal by the creators of the adaptation to the analogical mechanisms in the cultures of the East and West of the creation of a fairy-tale plot formation. This applies to both the characteristics of the model protagonists, and the domination of fantastic poetics in the development of the action—and there is also de-ritualization and de-sacralization (one form is the revelation of the "role" of the saintly author, who appears in the performance). This is why the language of the actors' stories is limited to the use of simple metonymy and synechdoche, based on the manipulation and transformation of everyday objects (which created the side effect of semanticization and desemanticization).[334]

---

[331] Brook interviewed by G. Banu, *The Language of Stories*, in: *Peter Brook and "The Mahabharata": Critical Perspectives*, ed. D. Williams, London 1990, 50.
[332] See D. Williams, *Theatre of Innocence…*, 23.
[333] P. Pavis, *Theatre at the Crossroads of Culture*, London and New York 1992, 187.
[334] See D. Williams, *The Great Poem of the World: A Descriptive Analysis*, in: *Peter Brook and "The Mahabharata": Critical Perspectives*, ed. idem, London 1990, 190.

As Eleazar Meletinsky wrote: "The fundamental moments in the process of the transformation of myth into tale are de-ritualization, secularization, the waning of faith in the veracity of mythical events, the development of a discourse of conscious invention, the loss of ethnographic specificity, the substitution of the mythical hero by the common man and of the mythical past by an indeterminate temporal dimension..."[335]

The effectiveness of the action of the fairy-tale, archetypal mechanism employed by Brook has been confirmed by, for example, Margaret Croyden, who wrote about "highly dramatic action rooted in Hindu culture and religion but at the same time archetypical and symbolic," conforming with the European morphology of the fairy tale: "There is the blind king, the ideal warrior, the devoted wife and many other mystic figures."[336]

Brook tried to turn the Indian myth, desacralized, into a universal fable. For this reason the style of the staging was supposed to be deliberately naive (in the sense of *art brut*), it was supposed to result from the mixing of convention, tradition, race, and culture and to appeal to an open style of acting, combining Brecht's alienation technique with Artaud's shock tactic; the adroitness of fabular narration with the hieratic physicality of the Asian theory of dance; the jester-like quality of caricatured humor with the dynamism and seriousness of the *theatrum militans*...[337]

In *Mahabharata*, Brook indeed created a new "intercultural" model of the work. The epic space and universalist interpretation enforce a sort of double, extensive reception of the action: in the context of the "great history of mankind" contained in the Hindu epos, and in the Shakespearian "theater of the world." The very making present of the action, on the other hand, creates a third variety of space: fairy-tale, de-sacralized, non-dramatic acting, above ritual and theater.

As Michael Billington wrote in this context, "If a general principle emerges, it is that human beings must find order within themselves to create an ordered universe."[338]

---

[335] E. M. Meletinsky, *The Poetics of Myth*, London and New York 2000, 237.
[336] M. Croyden, *Peter Brook Transforms*...
[337] See D. Williams, *Theatre of Innocence*..., 26.
[338] M. Billington, *Krishna Comes to the City*...

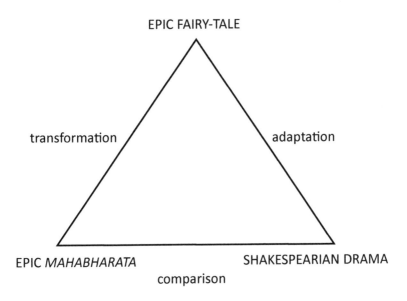

Figure 12. The "Intercultural" Model of Brook's *Mahabharata*

BEYOND UTOPIA AND FAITH: THE SPACE OF ANTI-ILLUSION

For Brook, the model for bestowing sense was a common nexus for both great traditions: the Eastern, inscribed in the *Mahabharata*, and the Western, identified with the Theater of Shakespeare. The model of stylistic homogeneity was the acceptance of a fairy-tale, archetypal convention that overwhelmed the audience.

Brook believed that the echoes of the cultural palimpsest (which India is often regarded as being, in the wake of a metaphor formulated by Nehru)[339] could be heard in the multicultural heterogeneity of the performance, created by the multilingual participants and co-creators of the whole undertaking.

In this fairy-tale-Shakespearian interpretation of *Mahabharata* lies the most dazzling realization of the idea of the de-limitation of culture in the twentieth century theater, where neither historical nor national conventions any longer determine the actual understanding between stage and audience, where a subconscious region of anthropological identity becomes the guarantee of "intercultural" understanding.

---

[339] D. Williams, *The Great Poem of the World...*, 191.

CONTINUITY REVOLUTIONS

Appearances to the contrary, the search for a New Theater in the 1960s and 1970s was not such a radical aesthetic turning point as at the turn of the nineteenth century. In the later version, the theatrical revolution was more concerned with rebellion against the existing culture (in the framework of the social phenomenon of the counterculture) and with short-term political objectives than with creating an enduring design for a new aesthetics that would last for more than a few theatrical seasons. There was more of a demand for an influence on revolutionary changes in politics seen in the short term than for the perfection of a theatrical reflection of the life of society. This led to widespread disenchantment on the part of participants in the whole movement, formulated as early as the seventies, that resulted from the failure of the new theater to meet hopes for a new social utopia.[340]

It is true that at the end of the twentieth century (as opposed to the situation a hundred years earlier) the pace was set by practitioners of the new theater who gave group and social characteristics to their productions under the banner of a change of generations. But in terms of the theory of the theater, as with social radicalism, there was a failure of endurance. Above all, there was no historic success in creating programs, postulates, and a vision.

When the utopian belief in the transformation of the world through theater, the creation of new social communities, and the transformation of audiences into revolutionary cultural or social formations weakened, it was noticed that there were many unexpected continuities, and sometimes surprising analogies, between the first and second editions of the quest

---

[340] See R. Schechner, *The Decline and Fall of the (American) Avant-Garde: Why It Happened and What We Can Do About It*, "Performing Arts Journal" 5 (2) (1981), 48–63.

for a New Theater. Once a summation of the theatrical experiments of the "counterculture" era began, it turned out that despite changes in language and acknowledged conventions and styles, the conceptual horizon had in fact altered very little since the days of the attempted reforming of the theater a hundred years earlier.

Feverishly making up (in theory as well!) for being more than a half century behind, Wilson seems with the demonstrated "visual musicality" of his Theater of Images to be the paradoxical successor to Appia; Kantor as the "constructor of emotions" in the Closed Theater and the Theater of Death could be seen as the paradoxical successor to Artaud; Brook with his epic and "intercultural" theater sanctified by ritual is obviously the paradoxical successor to Brecht.

The theater of the end of the twentieth century is the flickering out of a revolution; it is more a time of the practical realization and final definition of historical ideas than of the formulation of new, future-oriented postulates and programs.

CONCLUSION:
The dimensions of anti-illusion

Of the legacy of the quest for a New Theater at the turn of the nineteenth and twentieth centuries, there remains on the one hand an ideal model of the closed and repeatable authorial work that triumphs over its temporal nature. On the other hand, a competing model has been established of eternally incomplete communication and an open field of co-creation by many authors, including the audience. These opposed conventions have defined the boundaries of the contemporary theater, between creation and co-presence. Repeatedly destroyed in the cycle of "theatrical revolutions" but in fact indestructible, the box stage has immersed contemporary theater in insoluble spatial contradictions: open and closed, unity and diversity, secularity and the sacred, and above all, symmetry and asymmetry, the eternal order of the theatrical image and the living, thinking, feeling actor who shatters that order. The interplay between the sensual and illusory experience of limited, conventional space and the substantiality of the Other present in the here and now marks another theatrical boundary and has led over time to questions about the nature of the fleeting reality enclosed in the box, and also about the co-creative function of the audience, whose senses and experiences co-created the illusory—or disillusory—effect. Here, two model solutions have been possible: the truth of making-present or the convention of representation.

Post-Cartesian dualism imposed on modern drama the tension of the two theaters, the external and the internal. To grasp that tension it turned out to be necessary to relativize action understood in the Aristotelian sense, in favor of a subjective perspective, the introduction of epic commentary but also the allocation to the director of a privileged

CONCLUSION: The dimensions of anti-illusion

position as constructor of forms, marking out the frame and dynamics of changing situations, building the rhythm and tension. The coupling of "me—not me" finally objectivized the contemporary theater of alienation: in models of existential metaphor, in the limitation of the interpersonal to spontaneous speech acts, in attempts at the exploration of the human "primal substance" by the actors.

Literary theories of theater (rhetorical, Freytagian, phenomenological or semiotic) have endeavored to reduce the living play to a model of unchanging repeatability: the rhetorical pattern of ideal action, the principle of the "re-creation and representation" of appropriate layers of the drama, or rules for the "spatialization" of literature as a result of the necessary translation of a linguistic scenario into a multiplicity of spatio-temporal theatrical materials. The successes of these theories always had to do with the most formalized theatrical conventions (and thus those that were subordinated to literature). Yet the explosive dictionaries of signs and grammars of fables of the semantically frustrated European theater have never allowed anyone to forget about the opposite pole—its close associations with the practices of community life, which that theater had been trying for several centuries to imitate, merging its own rhetoric and the need for its social authentication into a bizarre unity.

Autonomic theories of theater (both modernistic and post-modern) sought a model outside literature and language—above all, they sought it in quasi-musical works which made possible the "permanent" designation of time, space, and the movement of the actor. On the other hand, there was an attempt to define and distinguish the supra-theatrical spectacle, engaging the participants (both individually and collectively) in a multi-morphic, multidimensional process. They postulated a movement away from *a priori*, model abstraction towards the magma of life, counting on a sometimes extreme relativism and the absolutization of the subconscious. Relativity, multiple perspectives, multivariance—these were the theater's new framework, negating the competence of any kind of super-arbiter equipped with the instruments of inquiry that could pin meanings in place. The latter, in the opinion of postmodernist anthropologists, can be extracted and isolated only by death, the only real closure and halting of the process, the only true boundary of theatricality.

CONCLUSION: The dimensions of anti-illusion

The history of the stage box—from its practical discovery by Renaissance painters through its definitive rejection in the post-naturalist phases of the New Theater—perpetuated the following exemplary antinomies of the theatrical performance:

1. in time—it revealed the conflict between the rhythmic order of the anthropocentric perspective and the regular variability of the location of the action on the one hand, and the arrhythmia of action and the feelings of the dramatic protagonists, ensnared in the unpredictability of the "interpersonal," on the other;
2. in space—the symmetry of a geometrical perspective, made visible within the framework of the stage on the model of a painting (according to the rules developed for two-dimensional images), contrasting with the asymmetrical network of symbolic meanings brought about by the three-dimensional actor;
3. in actions—the rigors of a mathematically conceived, artificially reproduced illusory world co-existed in conflict with events subordinated to a different pattern of geometrical abstraction.

The relative equilibrium of these antinomies constituted in essence a "box of illusion" up until the end of the nineteenth century and defined the rhetorical framework of the modern theater. The breaking of the box stage in the cycle of twentieth-century theatrical revolutions,[341] which required a Sisyphean effort, can be interpreted as an attempt at liquidating these antinomies in a situation where new aesthetic (anti-illusionism and the retreat from the domination by dramatic dialogue), social (the perfection of the theater as an instrument of effective influence), and psychological (the renunciation of the rationalization of space and the privileged direct contact between actor and audience) criteria no longer sufficed to justify them.

This also marked the end of "the two mathematical infinities" (the fruit of the perspective and Cartesian revolutions) and the beginning of a new tension between the chaos of what was outside and the abyss of what was inside the theatrical character (that phenomenon "created

---

[341] See D. Bablet, *La remise en question du lieu théâtral au vingtième siècle*, in: *Le lieu théâtral dans la société moderne*, réunies par D. Bablet, J. Jacquot, M. Oddon, Paris 1963, 13–25.

CONCLUSION: The dimensions of anti-illusion

in the image and likeness of man"[342]). The twentieth-century theater has fulfilled the aim of moving from a space that is a "mathematically accurate but psycho-physiologically impossible"[343] toward a space subjugated (in line with the development of cognition) to the ubiquity of "ordered disorder."[344] This is additionally explained by the need to "escape from illusion," understood as the re-creation and representation of the non-theatrical.

In the transformed box stage and in the proposed alternative theater place, on the ruins of the previously existing semiotics and rhetoric of "re-presentation," the twentieth century attempted to inscribe a new model of theatrical performance, in its assumptions an autonomous work definitively liberated from the rules of painting or literature although still—on the model of, for instance, music—vulnerable to the temptation of abstract, geometrical order[345]—an order no longer of copying, but of the composition, forms, and rhythms of action.

This, among other things, is what the explorations by the New Theater in the years 1887–1939 were about. The solutions arrived at in those years permanently changed the principle of theatrically making-present. They changed not the world but the self-sufficient work of theatrical art, or perhaps rather the message itself, into a closed feedback loop between stage and audience. Semioticians and structuralists concentrated on the formalized rules of the message sign, coming down on the side of the second of the competing concepts of the theatrical work as defined at the turn of the nineteenth and twentieth centuries. The phenomenologists and existentialists tracked down the rules for making-visible and making-present on stage "that which is theatrical," opting for the first concept: the absolute work itself in relation to its metaphysics. The sociologists and anthropologists in turn tried to unite both of these concepts into a system—limitless and unbounded—of references to the conventions of social life and intercultural patterns.

---

[342] Z. Raszewski, *Teatr w świecie...*, 61.
[343] A. Hauser, *The Social History...*, 69.
[344] See D. Peak, M. Frame, *Chaos Under Control: The Art and Science of Complexity*, New York 1994.
[345] See G. Arnoux, *Mathématique de la mise en scène*, Paris 1956.

CONCLUSION: The dimensions of anti-illusion

Jacques Derrida, so it would seem, grasped the ultimate consequences of the process that was taking place in the twentieth-century theater.[346] It was he who defined the theater of anti-illusion presence, understood as extra-textual deconstruction, an ontological manifesto of "unreal reality," an order beyond causality, and so on. But above all, he saw in the theater a model of the "space of indecision," illustrating the "impossibility of the unambiguous." This is the model that was used by the greatest theater artists of the late twentieth-century: Wilson, Brook, and Kantor (although none of them fits the formulas of post-modernism, not least in view of the purely modernistic faith in the exceptional mission of the artist and the sense of making art that they demonstrated, in opposition to electronic mass culture).

As much, then, as traditional illusion was a social category of the reception of the play, so contemporary anti-illusion turns out to be an individual psychological category of reaction to a play (no longer a spectacle, but activity, *performance*). Spatial anti-illusion is a result of the psychologization of the principles of theatrical convention, making them dependent on the direct relation of stage and audience. Anti-illusion is not merely a deliberate trick of the theater of the 1960s and 1970s, but rather a permanent element in the contemporary definition of theatricality reconciled to the traditional box stage (while for the reformers of the age of social ferment, the guarantee of anti-illusion was the abandonment not only of the frame of the box, but also of the closed space of the theatrical auditorium itself).

Perhaps this is why, years later, the explorations of the New Theater in the second half of the twentieth century seem to be merely a faint reflection of the explorations that marked the turn of the nineteenth and twentieth centuries, in changed social and civilizational conditions, in new times, when—in the theater, in literature, in culture, and in art—anti-illusion was widely accepted as a principle of cognition.

In the theater, the domination of the observing subject over the object of observation meant the privileging of the "fourth artist"—the beholder (as for example Meyerhold or Brecht would have it), or the beholder projecting the sense of the staging (as both the semioticians and

---

[346] E. Fuchs, *Presence and the Revenge...*, 163–173.

CONCLUSION: The dimensions of anti-illusion

the phenomenologists would have it). This is also an indirect argument for the indestructability of the "looking box," of utility both in creating visual illusions (in an analogy to the social image of the world) and in building alternative worlds (in an analogy to the anti-illusionistic rules of cognition).

In the twentieth century, together with the advance of science, there has been a lasting change in the hierarchy of the senses and the arts that correspond to them, a change in the rules for the visual reflecting of the world. Theater has ceased to be a mirror held up to reality, and has become a model part of reality. This has been facilitated by three dimensions of anti-illusion in theater at the close of the twentieth century:

1. in time: the collapse of tradition and the involvement in this—instead of in acting—of the protagonist; the destruction of the scenic form of the presentation and the involvement in this—instead of in creativity—of the director, actor and playwright; the scattering of formerly concentrated action in an unending spiral of possible context that goes beyond the frame of the performance—with the additional contribution of the spectators, whose participation is mandatory;

2. in space: the domination and unlimited nature of the "co-represented"; the paratheatrical and open-ended dialogue of the work and the idea (often only inventions that merely imitate ideas); autotelic conventions (in the relation of the theater to itself) instead of conventions of representation (in relation to the world), through the assertion that the only making-present of the subject may be a deconstructed form of presentation;

3. in the domain of action: the absence of an active individual, who has been replaced by an undefined collective subject (both the "transmitter of the play" and the audience invited to cooperation); the interplay of uncertainties on the ruins of the foundations of modern theater: actions that were once representational, present-oriented, and interpersonal; the seemingly unlimited play of the senses within the bounds of an intercultural collective: beyond cause, beyond the individual, finally beyond its historical time.

CONCLUSION: The dimensions of anti-illusion

It is hardly surprising that the main, and in fact the obsessive subject of the theater of the turn of the twentieth and twenty-first century is the polymorphous character of death: tradition and form, the protagonist and the world. Yet at the same time, there is a renewed shift toward theatrical practice, related (even if polemically) to the transformed, indestructible "box stage," a model of "pure" theatricality. This is another stage in the eternal struggle with the "literariness" of imitative action, with its unvarying hope for the achievement of the autonomy of the performance in formulas speaking, for instance, of the "theater of images"[347] (Wilson), "theater of memory" (Kantor), or "theater of naive experience" (Brook).[348] It is, finally, an incessant proposal to widen the frame of theatrical convention as non-mimetic space, a space of anti-illusion that sets free authentic, liberated performance, encompassing the whole of social life, from the confrontation with the naked reality of the objective world through the subjective, metaphysical experience of ritual.

---

[347] See B. Marranca (ed.), *The Theatre of Images*.
[348] See D. Williams, *Theatre of Innocence*...

BIBLIOGRAPHY

Abbott A. S., *The Vital Lie*, Tuscaloosa 1989.
Alberti L. B., *On Painting*, New Haven 1970.
Alter J., *A Socio-Semiotic Theory of Theatre*, Philadelphia 1990.
Appia A., *Staging Wagnerian Drama*, trans. P. Loeffler, Basel 1982.
Arens K., *Robert Wilson: Is Postmodern Performance Possible?*, "Theatre Journal" 1 (1991).
Arnheim R., *Art and Visual Perception: A Psychology of the Creative Eye*, Berkeley and Los Angeles 1974.
Arnoux G., *Mathématique de la mise en scène*, Paris 1956.
Artaud A., *On the Balinese Theater*, in: idem, *The Theater and Its Double*, trans. M. C. Richards, New York 1958.
Artaud A., *The Theater and Its Double*, trans. M. C. Richards, New York 1958.
Aslan O., *l'Acteur au XXe siècle*, Paris 1974.
Austin J. L., *How to Do Things With Words?*, Oxford 1962.
Austin J. L., *Sense and Sensibilia*, reconstructed from manuscript notes by G. J. Warnock, Oxford 1962.
Bablet D., *La mise en scène contemporaine. 1, 1887–1914*, Paris 1968.
Bablet D., *La remise en question du lieu théâtral au vingtième siècle*, in: *Le lieu théâtral dans la société moderne*, réunies par D. Bablet, J. Jacquot, M. Oddon, Paris 1963.
Banu G., *The Language of Stories*, in: *Peter Brook and "The Mahabharata": Critical Perspectives*, ed. D. Williams, London 1990.
Barba E., *Beyond the Floating Islands*, New York 1986.
Barba E., *Four Spectators*, "The Drama Review" 1 (1990).
Barba E., *The Paper Canoe*, London 1995.
Barba E., Savarese N., *A Dictionary of Theatre Anthropology: The Secret Art of the Performer*, London and New York 1991.

Bibliography

Barbour I. G., *Myths, Models and Paradigms: A Comparative Study in Science and Religion*, New York 1974.
Barish J., *The Antitheatrical Prejudice*, Berkeley 1985.
Barthes R., *Critical Essays*, trans. R. Howard, Evanston 1972.
Barthes R., *Littérature et signification*, "Tel Quel" (1963).
Barthes R., *The Structuralist Activity*, in: idem, *Critical Essays*, trans. R. Howard, Evanston 1972.
Barthes R., *The Tasks of Brechtian Criticism*, in: idem, *Critical Essays*, trans. R. Howard, Evanston 1972.
Béhar H., *Etude sur le théâtre dada et surréaliste*, Paris 1967.
Benamou M., Caramello C. (ed.), *Performance in Postmodern Culture*, Madison 1977.
Benveniste É., *Sémiologie de la langue*, "Semiotica" I, 1–2 (1969).
Berthold M., *A History of World Theater*, New York 1972.
Bharucha R., *Theatre and the World: Performance and the Politics of Culture*, London 1993.
Billington M., *I Is for Illusion*, "The Guardian" (February 8, 2012).
Billington M., *Krishna Comes to the City of the Popes*, "The Guardian" (July 16, 1983).
Błoński J., *Artaud i teatr magiczny*, in: A. Artaud, *Teatr i jego sobowtór*, trans. J. Błoński, Warszawa 1966.
Błoński J., *Peter Handke: przedmowa do teatru*, "Dialog" 6 (1969).
Błoński J., *Przedmowa*, in: J. L. Styan, *Współczesny dramat w teorii i scenicznej praktyce*, trans. M. Sugiera, Wrocław 1995.
Błoński J., *Teoria sytuacji dramatycznych Souriau*, "Dialog" 8 (1960).
Bogatyriew P., *Les signes au théâtre*, "Poétique" 8 (1971).
Bonnat Y., *Le décor de théâtre dans le monde depuis 1960*, Bruxelles 1973.
Borowski W., *Rozmowa z Tadeuszem Kantorem*, in: idem, *Kantor*, Warszawa 1982.
Brecht B., *A Short Organum for the Theatre*, in: *Brecht on Theatre*, ed. and trans. J. Willett, London 1974.
Brecht B., *Anmerkungen zur Oper „Aufstieg und Fall der Stadt Mahagonny,"* in: idem, *Gesammelte Werke*, Vol. 1, London 1958.
Brecht B., *Theatre for Pleasure or Theatre for Instruction*, in: *Twentieth Century Theatre: A Sourcebook*, ed. R. Drain, London 1995.
Brecht B., *Wartość mosiądzu*, trans. M. Kurecka, Warszawa 1975.

Britton D., *Theater, Popular and Special, and the Perils of Cultural Piracy*, in: *Peter Brook and "The Mahabharata": Critical Perspectives*, ed. D. Williams, London 1990.

Brook P., *The Presence of India: An Introduction*, in: *Peter Brook and "The Mahabharata": Critical Perspectives*, ed. D. Williams, London 1990.

Brook P., *The Empty Space: The Theatre Today*, London 1968.

Bürger P., *Theory of the Avant-Garde*, Manchester 1984.

Burns E., *Theatricality: A Study of Convention in the Theatre and in Social Life*, New York 1973.

Carlson M., *Theater as Event*, "Semiotica" 3–4 (1985).

Carlson M., *Theories of the Theatre*, Ithaka and London 1989.

Chomsky N., *Language and Mind*, New York 1968.

Connor S., *Postmodernist Culture: An Introduction to Theories of the Contemporary*, Oxford 1989.

Copeau J., *Texts on Theater*, ed. and trans. J. Rudlin and N. Paul, London 1990.

Corrigan R. W., *The Search for New Endings: The Theatre in Search of a Fix, Part III*, "Theatre Journal" 1 (1984).

Craig E. G., *On the Art of the Theater*, London 1911.

Craig E. G., *The Actor and the Über-marionette*, "The Mask" 1 (2) (April 1908).

Croyden M., *Peter Brook Transforms an Indian Epic for the Stage*, "The New York Times" (August 25, 1985).

Dasgupta G., *"The Mahabharata": Peter Brook's Orientalism*, in: *Interculturalism and Performance: Writings From PAJ [Performing Arts Journal]*, ed. B. Marranca, G. Dasgupta, New York 1991.

De Marinis M., *Capire il teatro. Lineamenti di una nuova teatrologia*, Firenze 1988.

De Monticelli R., *Sulla scena pasasano fantasmi d'avanguardia* (interview with T. Kantor), "Corriere della Sera" (January 29, 1978).

Deàk F., *Structuralism in Theatre: The Prague School Contribution*, "The Drama Review" 4 (1976).

Delsarte F., *Literary Remains of F. Delsarte*, in: *Delsarte System of Oratory*, New York 1893.

Dennett D., *Consciousness Explained*, Boston 1991.

Derrida J., *L'écriture et la différence*, Paris 1967.

Derrida J., *Writing and Difference*, Chicago 1978.

Durand R., *Problemes de l'analyse structurale et sémiotique de la forme théâtrale*, in: A. Helbo and others, *Sémiologie de la représentation. Théâtre, télévision, bande dessinée*, Bruxelles 1975.

Duvignaud J., *Les Ombres collectives*, Paris 1973.

Duvignaud J., *Spectacle et société*, Paris 1970.

Duvignaud J., Veinstein A., *Le théâtre*, Paris 1976.

Elam K., *Text Appeal and the Analysis Paralysis: Towards a Processual Poetics of Dramatic Production*, in: *Altro Polo Performance: From Product to Process*, ed. T. Fitzpatrick, Sydney 1989.

Elam K., *The Semiotics of Theatre and Drama*, London 1987.

Evreinov N., *Teatr kak takovoi*, Berlin 1923.

Fergusson F., *The Idea of a Theater*, New York 1955.

Fischer-Lichte E., *Geschichte des Dramas. Epochen der Identität auf dem Theater von der Antike bis zur Gegenwart*, Tübingen 1990.

Fischer-Lichte E., *Staging the Foreign as Cultural Transformation*, in: *The Dramatic Touch of Difference, Theatre, Own and Foreign*, ed. E. Fischer-Lichte, M. Gissenwehrer, J. Riley, Tübingen 1990.

Foakes R. A., *Making and Breaking Dramatic Illusion*, in: *Aesthetic Illusion Theoretical and Historical Approaches*, ed. F. Burwick, W. Pape, Berlin and New York 1990.

Förg G. (ed.), *Unsere Wagner: Joseph Beuys, Heinrich Müller, Karlheinz Stockausen, Hans-Jürgen Syberberg. Essays*, Frankfurt/M 1984.

Francastel P., *La Réalité figurative*, Paris 1965.

Franz M. L. von, *The Process of Individuation*, in: *Man and His Symbols*, ed. C. G. Jung, London 1979.

Freytag G., *Die Technik des Dramas*, Darmstadt 1965.

Freytag G., *Freytag's Techinique of the Drama: An Exposition and Art*, trans. and ed. E. J. MacEwan, Chicago 1894.

Fuchs E., *Presence and the Revenge of Writing: Re-thinking Theatre After Derrida*, "Performing Arts Journal" 2/3 (1985).

Fuchs G., *Die Revolution des Theaters*, München and Leipzig 1909.

Giraudet A., *Mimique, physionomie et geste*, Paris 1895.

Glover J. G., *The Cubist Theatre*, Michigan 1980.

Goffman E., *Interaction Ritual*, Garden City 1967.

Goffman E., *The Presentation of Self in Everyday Life*, Garden City 1959.

Goldberg R. L., *Performance: Live Art 1909 to the Present*, London 1979.

Gombrich E. H., *Art and Illusion: A Study in the Psychology of Pictorial Représentation*, London 1960.
Gouhier H., *Antonin Artaud et l'essence du théâtre*, Paris 1974.
Gouhier H., *L'Essence du théâtre*, Paris 1968.
Grotowski J., *Holiday (Święto): The Day That Is Holy*, in: *The Grotowski Sourcebook*, ed. R. Schechner, L. W. Wylam, London 1997.
Grotowski J., *Teksty z lat 1965–1969*, Wrocław 1989.
Hauser A., *The Social History of Art*, Vol. 2: *Renaissance, Mannerism, Baroque*, London and New York 1999.
Hawkes T., *Structuralism and Semiotics*, London 2003.
Holmberg A., *The Theatre of Robert Wilson*, Cambridge 1996.
Hornby R., *Script Into Performance: A Structuralist Approach*, New York 1987.
Ingarden R., *Sztuka teatralna, O funkcjach mowy w widowisku teatralnym*, in: *Problemy teorii dramatu i teatru*, ed. J. Degler, Wrocław 1988.
Ingarden R., *The Cognition of the Literary Work of Art*, Evanston 1979.
Jakobson R., *Two Aspects of Language and Two Type of Aphasic Disturbance*, in: R. Jakobson, M. Halle, *Fundamentals of Language*, The Hague 1956.
Jung C. G. (ed.), *Man and His Symbols*, London 1979.
Kantor T., *Miejsce teatralne*, in: idem, *Wielopole, Wielopole…*, Kraków 1984.
Kirby M., *Futurist Performance*, New York 1986.
Kolankiewicz L., *Święty Artaud*, Warszawa 1988.
Kolankiewicz L., *Teatr zarażony etnologią*, "Polska Sztuka Ludowa. Konteksty" 3–4 (1991).
Kowzan T., *Teatr jako uprzestrzennienie literatury*, "Dialog" 8 (1991).
Kowzan T., *The Sign in the Theater*, "Diogenes" 16 (61) (1968).
Lehmann H. T., *Postdramatic Theatre*, London and New York 2006.
Leonardo da Vinci, *The Treatise on Painting*, London 1877.
Lotman J. M., *Semiotyka sceny*, "Teatr" 1 (1980).
Lotman J. M., *Theater and Theatricality in the Order of Early Nineteenth Century Culture*, "Soviet Review" 16 (4) (1975).
Lotman J. M., Uspensky B. A., Mihaychuk G., *On the Semiotic Mechanism of Culture*, "New Literary History" 9 (2): *Soviet Semiotics and Criticism: An Anthology* (Winter, 1978).
Marranca B. (ed.), *The Theatre of Images*, New York 1996.

Bibliography

Mauron C., *Des métaphores obsédantes au mythe personnel. Introduction á la psychocritique*, Paris 1963.

Mehigan T. (ed.), *Frameworks, Artworks, Place: The Space of Perception in the Modern World*, Amsterdam 2008

Meletinsky E. M., *The Poetics of Myth*, London and New York 2000.

Meyerhold V., *The Reconstruction of the Theatre*, in: *Twentieth Century Theatre: A Sourcebook*, ed. R. Drain, London 1995

Miklaszewski K., *Encounters With Tadeusz Kantor*, London and New York 2002.

Morawski S., *Główne nurty estetyki XX wieku. Zarys syntetyczny*, Wrocław 1992.

Mukařovský J., *O jazyce básnickém*, "Slovo a slovenost" 3 (1940).

Müller G., *Dramaturgie des Theaters, des Horspiels und des Films*, Würzburg 1954.

O'Connor G., *The Mahabharata: Peter Brook's Epic in the Making*, London 1989.

Osiński Z., *Interakcja sceny i widowni w teatrze współczesnym*, in: *Wprowadzenie do nauki o teatrze*, Vol. 3, ed. J. Degler, Wrocław 1978.

Osolsobě I., *Zichova filozofie dramatického tvaru*, in: O. Zich, *Estetika dramatického umení*, Praha 1986.

Pavis P., *Dictionnaire du Théâtre*, Paris 1980.

Pavis P., *O semiologii inscenizacji*, trans. S. Świontek, in: *W kręgu zagadnień awangardy*, "Acta Universitatis Lodziensis. Folia Scientiarium Artium et Librorum" 3, ed. G. Gazda, R. W. Kluszczyński, Łódź 1982.

Pavis P., *Sémiologie théâtrale*, in: idem, *Dictionnaire du Théâtre*, Paris 1980.

Pavis P., *The Liberated Performance*, "Modern Drama" 1 (1982).

Pavis P., *Theatre at the Crossroads of Culture*, London and New York 1992.

Peak D., Frame M., *Chaos Under Control: The Art and Science of Complexity*, New York 1994.

Peter J., *Vladimir's Carrot: Modern Drama and the Modern Imagination*, London 1987.

Pleśniarowicz K., *The Dead Memory Machine: Tadeusz Kantor's Theatre of Death*, trans. W. Brand, Aberystwyth 2004.

Propp V., *Morphology of the Folktale*, trans. L. Scott, ed. L. A. Wagner, Austin 1968.

Quigley A. E., *The Modern Stage and Other Worlds*, New York and London 1985.

Raszewski Z., *Krótka historia teatru polskiego*, Warszawa 1977.

Raszewski Z., *Partytura teatralna*, "Pamiętnik Teatralny" 3–4 (1958).

Raszewski Z., *Przedmowa*, in: J. Furttenbach, *O budowie teatrów*, trans. Z. Raszewski, Wrocław 1958.

Raszewski Z., *Teatr w świecie widowisk*, Warszawa 1991.

Raszewski Z., *Wstęp*, in: A. Appia, *Żywa sztuka czy martwa natura?...*, "Pamiętnik Teatralny" 4 (1956).

Ratajczak D., *Przestrzeń w dramacie i dramat w przestrzeni teatru*, Poznań 1985.

Ruffini F., *Semiotica del teatro, I–III*, "Biblioteca Teatrale" 9 (1974); 10/11 (1975); 14 (1976).

Ruffini F., *The Culture of the Text and the Culture of the Stage*, in: E. Barba, N. Savarese, *A Dictionary of Theater Anthropology: The Secret Art of the Performer*, London and New York 1991.

Schechner R., *Between Theater and Anthropology*, Philadelphia 1985.

Schechner R., *News, Sex and Performance Theory*, in: *Innovation/Renovation: New Perspectives in the Humanities*, ed. I. Hassan, S. Hassan, Madison 1983.

Schechner R., *Performance Theory*, New York and London 1988.

Schechner R., *The Decline and Fall of the (American) Avant-Garde: Why It Happened and What We Can Do About It*, "Performing Arts Journal" 5 (2) (1981).

Schechner R., *The Performer: Training Interculturally*, "Canadian Theatre Review" 35 (1982).

Sebeok T. A., *Iconicity*, "MLN" 91 (6): *Comparative Literature* (December 1976).

Sinko G., *Opis przedstawienia teatralnego. Problem semiotyczny*, Wrocław 1982.

Skwarczyńska S., *Znaki teatralne i fraza w komunikacie teatralnym o fabule dramatycznej*, in: eadem, *W orbicie literatury, teatru, kultury naukowej*, Warszawa 1985.

Sławiński J., *Dzieło. Język. Tradycja*, Warszawa 1974.

Sławkowie E. and T., *Teatr filozofii*, "Teatr" 1 (1988).

Smith J. S., *A Theory of Drama and Theatre: A Continuing Investigation of the Aesthetics of Roman Ingarden*, "Analecta Husserliana" 33 (1991).

Souriau É., *Les Deux cent mille situations dramatiques*, Paris 1950.

Souriau É., *Les Grands problèmes de l'esthétique théâtrale*, Paris 1963.

Stanislavsky C., *My Life in Art*, London 1924.

Steinbeck D., *Einleitung in die Theorie und Systematik der Theaterwissenschaft*, Berlin 1970.

Styan J. L., *Modern Drama in Theory and Practice*, Vol. 1: *Realism and Naturalism*, Vol. 2: *Symbolism, Surrealism and the Absurd*, Vol. 3: *Symbolism, Expressionism and Epic Theatre*, Cambridge 1986.
Suvin D., *To Brecht and Beyond: Soundings in Modern Dramaturgy*, Brighton 1984.
Szondi P., *Theory of the Modern Drama*, ed. and trans. M. Hays, Cambridge 1987.
Tharu S. J., *The Sense of Performance: Studies in Post-Artaud Theatre*, New Delhi 1984.
Thomas D., *Embodied Phenomenology*, "Journal of Literary Semantics" 42 (1) (January 2013).
Tischner J., *Filozofia dramatu. Wprowadzenie*, Paris 1990.
Turner V., *From Ritual to Theatre: The Human Seriousness of Play*, New York 1982.
Turner V., *The Anthropology of Performance*, New York 1988.
Ubersfeld A., *Lire le théâtre*, Paris 1978.
Valency M., *The End of World: An Introduction to Contemporary Drama*, Oxford 1980.
Virmaux A., *Antonin Artaud et le théâtre*, Paris 1970.
Watson I., *Toward a Third Theatre: Eugenio Barba and the Odin Teatret*, London 1993.
Wellwarth G. E., *Modern Drama and the Death of God*, Madison 1986.
Whyman R., *The Stanislavsky System of Acting: Legacy and Influence in Modern Performance*, Cambridge 2011.
Williams D. (ed.), *Peter Brook and "The Mahabharata": Critical Perspectives*, London 1990.
Williams D., *The Great Poem of the World: A Descriptive Analysis*, in: *Peter Brook and "The Mahabharata": Critical Perspectives*, ed. idem, London 1990.
Williams D., *Theatre of Innocence and of Experience: Peter Brook's International Centre: An Introduction*, in: *Peter Brook and "The Mahabharata": Critical Perspectives*, ed. idem, London 1990.
Wilshire B., *Role Playing and Identity: The Limits of Theatre as Metaphor*, Bloomington 1982.
Wilson R., *Preface*, in: *The Theatre of Images*, ed. B. Marranca, New York 1996.
Wittkower R., *Architektural Principles in the Age of Humanism*, London 1949.

Wolf W., *Illusion and Breaking Illusion in Twentieth-Century Fiction*, in: *Aesthetic Illusion Theoretical and Historical Approaches*, ed. F. Burwick, W. Pape, Berlin and New York 1990.

Wołkoński S., *Człowiek wyrazisty. Sceniczne wychowanie gestu (według Delsarte'a)*, Warszawa 1920.

Wyka K., *Modernizm polski*, Kraków 1968.

Yates F. A., *The Art of Memory*, London 1992.

Zich O., *Estetika dramatického umení*, Praha 1986.

Ziomek J., *Powinowactwo przez fabułę*, in: idem, *Powinowactwa literatury*, Warszawa 1980.

INDEX

Abbott Anthony S. 140
Alberti Leon Battista 15, 17
Alter Jean 135
Antoine André 8, 47, 48, 59
Appia Adolphe 10, 45, 49–59, 63, 70, 76, 81, 85, 168
Arens Katherine 141
Aristotle 34, 38, 76, 87, 88, 104, 131
Arnheim Rudolf 16, 19, 28, 40, 42
Arnoux Georges 172
Artaud Antonin 10, 45, 57–69, 76, 80, 81, 85, 139, 141, 142, 146, 158, 164, 168
Aslan Odette 29, 32, 67–69
Austin John L. 20, 95, 96

Bablet Denis 45, 46, 48, 171
Banu Georges 163
Barba Eugenio 95, 124–128, 140, 159
Barbour Ian G. 9
Barish Jonas A. 119
Barthes Roland 9, 10, 80, 91, 98, 141
Beck Julian 126, 140
Beckett Samuel 58
Beethoven Ludwig van 133
Béhar Henri 59
Benamou Michel 139
Benveniste Émile 89

Bergson Henri 66
Berthold Margot 18
Beuys Joseph 142
Bharucha Rustom 160, 161
Billington Michael 7, 161, 164
Błoński Jan 46, 60, 63, 67, 95, 103
Bogatyriew Petr 90
Bonnat Yves 120
Borowski Wiesław 148
Brand William 147
Brecht Bertolt 10, 72, 74–81, 85, 104, 139, 164, 168, 173
Britton David 163
Brook Peter 11, 58, 102, 126, 140, 158–166, 168, 173, 175
Bürger Peter 154
Burns Elizabeth 41, 115, 120–123, 135
Burwick Frederick 8, 9

Caramello Charles 139
Carlson Marvin 26, 35, 130
Carrière Jean Claude 161
Chekhov Anton 35
Chekhov Mikhail 26
Chomsky Noam 132
Christoph Friedrich von 35
Cicero Marcus Tullius 26

Index

Claudel Paul 104
Connor Steven 139
Copeau Jacques 70, 81, 102
Corneille Pierre 21
Corrigan Robert W. 141
Cousin Victor 29
Craig Edward Gordon 8, 45, 49, 50, 58, 59, 69, 70, 81, 116
Crémieux Benjamin 46
Croyden Margaret 159, 160, 164

Dante Alighieri 133
Dasgupta Gautam 160
De Marinis Marco 94
Deák František 88
Degler Janusz 90, 102
Delsarte François 25–32
Dennett Daniel 21
Derrida Jacques 66, 139, 141, 146, 173
Descartes René 20, 21, 67, 130, 131
Diderot Denis 122
Drain Richard 72, 74
Durand Regis 10
Duvignaud Jean 24, 119, 120

Eco Umberto 94
Einstein Albert 141
Elam Keir 87, 88, 91, 92, 95
Esslin Martin 80
Estienne Marie-Hélène 162
Evreinov Nikolai 70, 71

Fergusson Francis 103
Fischer-Lichte Erika 140, 162

Fitzpatrick Tim 95
Foakes Reginald A. 7, 8
Förg Gabriele 142
Frame Michael 172
Francastel Pierre 7
Franz Marie-Louise von 152
Freytag Gustav 35–38, 41, 104, 117, 170
Fuchs Elinor 141, 173
Fuchs Georg 70
Furttenbach Joseph 16

Galileo 76
Gazda Grzegorz 91
Genet Jean 58
Giraudet Alfred 30, 31
Gissenwehrer Michael 162
Glover Joseph Garrett 50
Goethe Johann Wolfgang von 35
Goffman Erving 121, 131, 132
Goldberg Rose Lee 50
Gombrich Ernst Hans 25
Gombrowicz Witold 147
Gouhier Henri 36, 66, 104, 105, 135, 147
Grotowski Jerzy 32, 46, 56, 66, 102, 124, 126, 140, 159

Halle Morris 157
Handke Peter 103, 140
Hassan Ihab 141
Hassan Sally 141
Hauptmann Gerhart Johann Robert 35
Hauser Arnold 18, 20, 40, 172
Hawkes Terence 85, 87, 94
Hegel Georg Wilhelm Friedrich 131

Helbo André 10
Holmberg Arthur 144
Homer 133
Hornby Richard 85
Howard Richard 10, 80, 98
Husserl Edmund 108

Ibsen Henrik 35, 46
Ingarden Roman 102, 105–109, 135
Irving Henry 8

Jacquot Jean 171
Jakobson Roman 92, 157
Jaques-Dalcroze Émile 56
Jarry Alfred 58, 59
Jung Carl Gustav 152

Kandinsky Wassily 142
Kant Immanuel 131
Kantor Tadeusz 10, 116, 140, 147–149, 151–155, 157, 168, 173, 175
Kirby Michael 50
Knowles Christopher 143
Kolankiewicz Leszek 60, 126
Kowzan Tadeusz 91, 92, 95, 96, 135, 147
Krejča Ottomar 159

Laughton Charles 76
Lehmann Hans-Thies 140
Leonardo da Vinci 27, 42, 133
Lessing Gotthold Ephraim 25, 32, 35
Lévi-Strauss Claude 94
Loeffler Michael Peter 52
Lotman Jurij M. 34, 89, 91, 92, 97, 98
Lugné-Poe Aurélien 49, 59

MacEwan Elias J. 36
Maeterlinck Maurice 139
Malina Judith 126, 140
Marranca Bonnie 141–144, 146, 160, 175
Mauron Charles 151, 152
Mehigan Tim 56
Meletinsky Eleazar 164
Meyerhold Vsevolod 26, 71–73, 78, 81, 173
Michaelangelo 28
Mihaychuk George 89
Miklaszewski Krzysztof 149
Millon Martine 160
Mnouchkine Ariane 140
Molière 36
Monticelli Roberto de 148
Morawski Stefan 89
Mrożek Sławomir 104
Mukařovský Jan 87–89, 96
Müller Gottfried 35
Müller Heinrich 142

Nehru Jawaharlal 166
Noverre Jean 25

O'Connor Garry 161
Oddon Marcel 171
Osiński Zbigniew 90
Osolsobě Ivo 97

Pape Walter 8, 9
Paul Norman H. 102
Pavis Patrice 8, 88, 91, 95, 141, 163
Peak David 172

Index

Peirce Charles Sanders 90, 94
Peter John 140
Pinter Harold 140
Pirandello Luigi 58
Plato 34, 131, 133
Pleśniarowicz Krzysztof 147, 153
Propp Vladimir 94

Quigley Austin E. 9, 140

Racine Jean 22
Raszewski Zbigniew 16, 18, 20, 41, 55, 57, 109–118, 135, 136, 172
Ratajczak Dobrochna 16, 18–20, 22–24, 34
Reinhardt Max 46
Riccoboni Antonio Francesco 122
Richards Mary Caroline 58, 61
Riley Josephine 162
Rousseau Jean-Jacques 119
Rudlin John 102
Ruffini Franco 92, 94, 95

Sardou Victorien 36
Saussure Ferdinand de 86
Savarese Nicola 95, 127
Schechner Richard 41, 56, 85, 124, 125, 129–132, 141, 167
Schiller Friedrich 35
Schlemmer Oskar 81, 85
Schulz Bruno 147
Scott Laurence 94
Sebeok Thomas A. 90
Seweryn Andrzej 160

Shakespeare William 35, 38, 71, 103, 104, 133, 158, 159, 162, 163, 166
Sinko Grzegorz 93
Skwarczyńska Stefania 93, 94
Sławek Ewa 139
Sławek Tadeusz 139
Sławiński Janusz 87, 89
Smith Jadwiga S. 105
Sophocles 35, 41
Souriau Étienne 95, 96, 102
Stanislavski Konstantin (Stanisławski) 8, 26, 48, 81, 85
Steinbeck Dietrich 107, 109
Stoppard Tom 140
Strehler Giorgio 140
Strindberg August 8, 35, 104
Styan John L. 8, 46, 58, 72, 80
Sugiera Małgorzata 46
Suvin Darko 140
Syberberg Hans-Jürgen 142
Szondi Peter 34, 35, 46, 75, 104

Świontek Sławomir 91

Tharu Susie J. 22
Thomas Dylan 42
Tischner Józef 108
Turner Victor 124, 130, 132, 133

Ubersfeld Anne 105, 106
Uspenskij Boris 89

Vakhtangov Yevgeny 26
Valency Maurice 140
Veinstein André 24
Virmaux Alain 59

Index

Vitruvius 30
Volkonsky Sergey (Wołkoński Sergiusz) 25–29, 32

Wagner Richard 46, 50, 52–58, 73, 94, 142, 146
Wardle Irving 159
Warnock Geoffrey James 20
Watson Ian 126
Weiss Peter 140
Wellwarth George E. 140
Whyman Rose 26
Willett John 76
Williams David 161–163, 166, 175
Wilshire Bruce 108, 109

Wilson Robert 10, 140–146, 173, 175
Witkacy, Witkiewicz Stanisław Ignacy 147, 151, 155, 156
Wittgenstein Ludwig 96
Wittkower Rudolf 41
Wyka Kazimierz 47
Wylam Lisa Wolford 56
Wyspiański Stanisław 58, 85

Yates Frances A. 30, 41
Yeats William Butler 139

Zhdanov Andrey 80
Zich Otakar 88, 96–101
Ziomek Jerzy 116

Editor
Zofia Sajdek

Proofreading
Małgorzata Zelek-Łata

Typesetting
Wojciech Wojewoda

Jagiellonian University Press
Editorial Offices: Michałowskiego 9/2, 31-126 Kraków, Poland
Phone: +48 12 663 23 80